Please read this first

We require that you call us to report any damaged or missing items within 72 hours of delivery.

To take full advantage of your computer, you will need:

- A high-speed Internet connection from an Internet Service Provider (ISP) such as Comcast, Verizon, or Clear
- An e-mail account including your username and password

If you DO NOT have an Internet connection…

You can proceed with setup but be aware that you will not be able to enjoy the following features until an Internet connection is available:

- Email
- Photo Sharing
- Web Browsing
- Video Chat
- News
- Weather

If you DO have an Internet connection and an e-mail account…

Congratulations! You are only a few steps away from enjoying sharing family photos, and surfing your favorite web sites. Please go to Step 1 on page 5.

Cleaning Guidelines

If you wish to clean your computer screen, you can use the enclosed LCD Display Wiper or a dry, clean, lint-free cotton cloth. Or, if you wish to use a liquid cleaner it must not be ammonia based. Apply the cleaner lightly to a clean, lint-free cloth and then wipe the screen. Do not allow any liquid to drip on the screen.

Caution

You may use commercial keyboard cleaners available at consumer electronics stores. Never pour liquid into the keyboard or immerse the keyboard in any liquid.

Table of Contents

Telikin Quick Start Guide 4
    Step 1: Know the Parts 4
    Step 2: Unpack and Prepare your Telikin 5
    Step 3: Connect Power to your Telikin 6
    Step 4: Connect your Telikin to the Internet 7
    Step 5: Powering on your Telikin 8
    Step 6: Configuring your Telikin 9
    Step 7: Key Usage Features 11
    Step 8: Documentation and Support 12
    Step 9: Printer Information... 13
    Step 10: Packing Guidelines 14

User's Manual 15
    Getting Started 16
    Overview 19
    Home 22
    Video Chat 24
    Email Inbox 28
    Composing an Email 31
    Reading an Email 33
    Saving Email Attachments 34
    Photos 36
    My Albums 37
    Viewing and Managing Photos.. 39
    Thumbnail View 43
    Calendar 43
    Contacts 45
    Weather 49
    News 50
    Web 52
    Games 54

More	54
Backup/Restore	55
CD Player	57
Calculator	59
Conversion	60
DVD Player	60
File Manager	61
Kindle Reader	64
Media Player	67
PDF Viewer	71
Scanner	73
Slideshow Viewer	75
Spreadsheets	76
Stopwatch	80
Timer	81
Write	81
My Profile Settings	84
User Accounts	85
Video Chat Settings	89
Email Settings	90
Facebook Settings	94
System Info	94
System Settings	96
Print Settings	97
Network Settings	100
Tech Buddy Settings	103
Browser Settings	105
Telikin Standard Product Warranty	**110**
End User License Agreement (EULA)	**112**
Save Your Account Information	**117**

Copyright 2012 • Venture 3 Systems LLC. • Chalfont, PA

Telikin Quick Start Guide
Step 1: Know the Parts

❶ Power indicator light
❷ Power button
❸ Power adapter inlet
❹ USB ports (for keyboard & Mouse)
❺ Network port
❻ SD memory card slot
❼ CD/DVD tray
❽ Screen Setting controls (Factory Set)

Step 2: Unpack and Prepare your Telikin

Carefully remove all pieces from the box and place on a flat surface.

Please retain all boxes and packing materials in the event that you need to invoke your warranty.

The factory packaging has been specifically designed, and approved by UPS to provide maximum protection during shipping.

Verify you have all items on your order before proceeding.

If any part is missing or damaged, contact Customer Support.

Connect the keyboard and mouse to the USB ports at the back of the device (See page 4 for location).

Look for the plugs with this symbol on them:

Step 3: Connect Power to your Telikin

Connect the power cord and adapter together as shown.

Connect the power adapter* to the inlet at the back of the device (see page 4 for location).

You can plug the power cord into a convenient wall outlet; however, to avoid damage to the computer, and comply with the warranty terms, it is recommended that you use a UL approved power strip with a surge protector (as shown).

* Use only the supplied adapter to apply power to your Telikin. Using anything other than the supplied adapter could damage your computer.

Step 4: Connect your Telikin to the Internet

Tech Tip: Calling our support line while the Internet Installation Technician is at your residence will simplify the installation and activation of your internet service.

If you plan to use a wireless (WiFi) Internet connection, continue on to step 5.

Using the supplied network cable, connect one end to the network port at the back of the device (see page 4 for location).

Connect the other end to the network port of your cable modem or other Internet device.

Note: Before proceeding to the next section, make sure your cable modem or other Internet device is powered on.

Tech Tip: If a wired network connection is available we recommend using it to ensure the best possible computing experience.

Tech Tip: If you need a longer Ethernet cable, you can purchase one at a consumer electronics store.

Step 5: Powering on your Telikin

Facing the computer screen, press the power button on the right side of the device (see page 4 for location).

You can power off the Telikin by tapping the same power button, or (preferred) from the **Home** screen, click **Settings** then **Power Off**.

When powered on, the power indicator light on the front of the device will be illuminated (see page 4 for location).

Optional external speakers can be attached to the speaker connector as shown at left.

Troubleshooting

- If the power indicator is not illuminated, please start by checking the power light indicator on the power adapter connected to the wall outlet (see page 4 for location). Make sure the outlet (or power strip) is not switched off.

- If the light on the power adapter is not illuminated, please make sure the power cord is pushed tightly into the power adapter.

- If the power indicator on the power adapter is illuminated and the power indicator on the front of the device is not, please contact customer support.

Step 6: Configuring your Telikin

Once your Telikin is powered on, you will see the End User License Agreement (EULA). This is an agreement that is customary for software. It states that you agree to only use the software on one computer and not make copies of the software. Please read the EULA and click the check box at the bottom left to agree. Once you agree, The EULA will not be shown again and you will be taken to the **Home** screen.

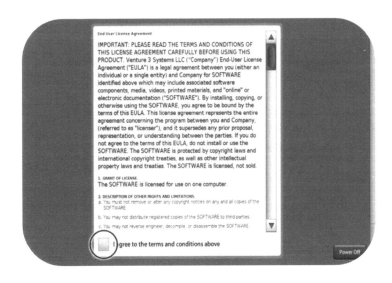

On the **Home** screen, the **Notices** panel will contain a list of items that you can click to easily setup some of your personal information. You will see some or all of the following phrases:

"Click to set up your Network"

Click this message to view the Network/Internet Settings page to see network connection status or connect to a wireless network. You will not see this message if you are successfully connected to the Internet. To get to the Network/Internet Settings page, click **Home**, then click **Settings**, and then click **Network Settings**.

If you are using an Ethernet cable to connect to the internet, the **Wired Network** section will show Ethernet **Status** as "Connected". If this status is "Not Connected", check your wired connections – alternately, if you are using DSL internet service, it may need to be activated. Please call us for help with activation.

If you will be using a wireless connection to the internet, the **Wireless Networks** section will list available networks. Find your wireless network name in the list and click the **Connect** button for this network in the **Status** column. If your network requires a password, enter it in the **Wireless Network Configuration** screen and click **Ok, Try to Connect** (the password will be supplied by your internet provider – or may be on the bottom of your modem). Your computer will then attempt to connect to your wireless network. When connected, the status will change to "Connected". Write down your network name and network password on the last page of this book.

"Click to set up your User Profile"

The profile will be used to personalize your Telikin for local weather (zip code), as well as allow it to maintain your address, birthday, and other contact information for your virtual address book.

Enter your personal information in the text fields given and then click **Save Changes**.

"Click to set up your E-mail account"

- If you already have an e-mail address (i.e. "YourName@gmail.com")…

Please enter it & your password into the provided fields and click **Save**.

Note: YAHOO! free email accounts DO NOT support POP or IMAP protocols through 3rd party email clients such as Outlook, Outlook Express, and the Telikin email client. Therefore it is suggested to use Gmail or similar accounts.

- If you do not have an e-mail address…

You can create your own e-mail account using any online service such as Gmail or Hotmail. Once you have your e-mail account information, please enter it into the provided fields and click **Save**.

Write down your e-mail address and password on the last page of this book.

Time Zone Settings

To set your time zone, from the **Home** screen, click the **Settings** button, then click the **System Settings** button. If you are not yet connected to the Internet, or do not plan to connect to the internet, click the **Set Time** button to set the time manually. Otherwise, select your time zone from the list. Once your computer is connected to the Internet, the exact time will be obtained the next time the computer is turned on.

Congratulations! You have successfully setup your Telikin!

You can now enjoy the easy-to-use, friendly features that will keep you connected to friends and family around the world!

Step 7: Key Usage Features

Volume and Magnification Features

Located at the top right side of your screen is the **Volume** button. Click this button to display a bar with a slider. Click and drag the slider up or down to raise or lower the volume level.

To the right of the **Volume** button is the **Magnifier** button. Click this button to open a magnifying window. Move the window to magnifier areas of the screen. The cursor is now located in the center of the magnifier window. To disable the magnifier, press the escape (Esc) key on your keyboard, or center the magnifier over the **Magnifier** button and click the button.

Step 8: Documentation and Support

User Manual & Video Tutorials

A copy of this User Manual is also built right into your computer!

To get started, click the **Help** button, located at the top, right corner of the screen. This opens the **Help** window, where you can read or watch video tutorials. To enlarge the screen, click the **Maximize** button.

Click the **Index** button to pop out the **Table of Contents**. Click any chapter to "go" to that chapter.

To watch a video tutorial, click the **Video** button. Click **Text** to return to the written manual.

Click the **Close** button to close the **Help** window. If you click another blue application button – or any of the settings buttons – and then click the **Help** button again, it will open to that chapter in the manual.

Messages from Us

Occasionally, we will want to share important information with you about your computer. When we do, you'll see this notice on the **Home** screen: "You have one message from Support". Click this notice to view the message. To re-read a message, or read past messages, click **Help**, then click **Messages**.

Email Support

To send an email to Support, please follow these steps:

1. Click **Help**
2. Click **Contact Support** – this opens an email form
3. Complete the form fields and click **Send**

Step 9: Printer Information

In order to ensure an easy "plug and print" experience, we currently only support Hewlett Packard (HP) printers that connect to your computer with a USB cable.

If your computer is connected to the internet, you can easily determine if a particular HP printer is fully compatible.

Check Printer Compatibility

Click **Home**, then click **Settings**, and then click **Print Settings**. Next click the **Help** button, (you may wish to click the Maximize button to enlarge the Help window). Skip to the **Supported Printers** section that describes how to look up a printer.

Please call Customer Support if you'd like to check the compatibility of a specific HP printer model.

Printer Setup

To setup your printer there is no need to install any printer driver software, as HP drivers are already installed on the computer. Follow these steps to connect and install your printer:

- Plug in the power cables, connect to power and turn on the printer
- Load the paper according to the printer manual
- Open the cartridge door and install the printer cartridges according to the printer manual
- Close the cartridge door and plug the printer's USB cable into the printer and the other end of the cable into one of the USB ports at the back or side of your computer (see page 4 for location)
- Turn your computer on

Printing a Test Page

From the **Home** screen, click **Settings**, then click **Print Settings**, and then click **Print Test Page**.

Step 10: Packing Guidelines

Step 1 – Place accessory items in the Power Supply box.

- Power Adapter
- Stylus
- Mouse in Mouse Box
- Screen Cleaning Cloth
- Power cord

Step 2 – Place the foam protectors on the Telikin.
Step 3 – Place the Telikin in the box.

- Foam protector
- Mouse/Power Supply box
- Telikin (front faces tabs)
- Place NOTHING in front of the screen

Step 4 – Place the Power Supply box between the foam protectors behind the Telikin and slide it to the bottom of the box.

Keyboard in box

Step 5 – Place the keyboard box in between the foam protectors and above the Power Supply box, then close the box.

Telikin
User's Manual

Getting Started

Introduction

Hello and congratulations on the purchase of your computer! In order to control your computer and tell it what to do next, you will need to learn how to use the mouse or touchscreen and the keyboard. In this tutorial, we go over the basic skills of using the mouse, the keyboard and the touch screen, as well as getting help. Let's get started!

We have made this information available to you in a video tutorial. If you would like to watch it, click the Video button at the top of this window. To end the video, click the Text button at the top of this window.

The Mouse

Holding the Mouse

The mouse is a useful device. It fits in the palm of your hand and gives you direct control of your computer screen. The mouse movement directly correlates to the movement of the pointer on the screen (the pointer is shaped like a small triangle). If you move the mouse to the right with your hand, the pointer will also move to the right. If you move the mouse in circles, you will see the pointer move in circles too.

Like any other tool, you'll want to practice using the mouse to get the feel of it and be able to use it comfortably.

To begin using the mouse, lay it on a flat surface close to the right side of the computer. Position the mouse so that the wire facing away from you and plugged into the back or side of the computer. Next, lay your right hand on top of the mouse. Its curved shape should fit comfortably in your palm, with your fingers draped down over the front of the mouse toward the wire.

The mouse has 2 buttons - a left and a right button, located on the top of the mouse. When you place your right hand on the mouse, your index finger will be on the left mouse button and your middle finger will be on the right mouse button. You may need to adjust your fingers to position them in this way.

Using the Mouse

You use the mouse to you control your computer and tell it what to do next. Using the mouse is a two-step process: first you move the mouse to position the pointer on the computer screen, and then use your index finger to click the left mouse button. We call this a click because your mouse will make a click sound when you press down on it. From now on we will refer to clicking on the left mouse button as a "click". Clicking on the right mouse button is described below and will be referred to as a "right-click". You may want to practice moving the mouse to see how the pointer on the screen moves with it. Practicing moving the mouse and using the left mouse click with your index finger will help improve your hand-eye coordination.

Mouse Right-Click

For the most part, you will not have to use the button located on the right side of your mouse. Right-clicking is also a two-step process: you position the pointer by moving the mouse and then click down with your middle finger. Right-clicking, as it's called, is used for two functions in your computer: 1) spell correction and 2) saving images.

Spell Correction

Spell correction is available in the Email and Write applications. While typing, if you misspell a word, it will appear with a red squiggly line under it. To correct the misspelled word, simply move the mouse so the pointer is on top of the misspelled word and click the right mouse button with your middle finger. This will prompt the Spell Check feature, which will open a window with several spelling suggestions. Simply click the checkbox next to the correctly spelled word and then click OK to use it.

Scroll Bars

Often, when you view information on your computer, there may be more pages than will fit on the screen. If you were viewing a book, you would turn the page. On your computer, you will need to "scroll" to see more. To scroll, you will need to learn how to use scroll bars.

Scroll bars are used to move between pages in large documents or websites. Scroll bars can be used to scroll vertically, up and down, through multiple pages, or horizontally, back and forth, across wide pages. Basically, scrolling is used to adjust the viewing area on the screen so you can read and see content that extends beyond the viewing area of your computer screen.

Your computer will sense when there is not enough room to display all the pages or content, and display scroll bars automatically on the computer screen.

Using Scroll Bars

Using a scroll bar is a two-step process: first you position the mouse over the slider - the blue rectangle inside the scrolling area - then you click down and hold the button down while moving the mouse. For vertical scroll bars, you'll move the mouse in an up/down motion. For horizontal scroll bars, you'll move the mouse in a left/right motion. Moving the slider will scroll the document in the direction you move the mouse. You can let go of the mouse button when you have reached the area of the page you want to view.

Scrolling allows you to move quickly through pages. If you want to move one line at a time, click the blue arrow buttons located at the top and bottom of the scroll bar.

The Keyboard

You will use your keyboard whenever typing is required by your computer. The keyboard contains keys marked with letters, numbers and symbols. When you press a key, the character marked on that key is typed.

Keyboard Arrangement

Your keyboard is laid out in the QWERTY format. The name comes from the leftmost, top five /letters on the keyboard.

The middle section of your keyboard contains letters. Above the letters you will see a row of numbers. The longest key at the bottom of your keyboard is the space bar. This inserts spaces when you are typing. The Enter or Return key is used to insert a new line when moving to the next paragraph.

Common Keys

Here is an explanation of the most used keys on the keyboard.

- Backspace: Erases typed characters to the left of the cursor.
- Caps Lock: Turns on or off CAPITALIZATION. When on, a lighted A appears at the top center of the keyboard (9). Press Caps Lock again to turn it off.
- Control: Used in combination with other keys to perform special functions.
- Delete: Erases typed characters to the right of the cursor.
- Enter / Return: Inserts a new, blank line. Equivalent to a carriage return on a typewriter.
- Function Keys: These are presently unused.
- Insert: Switches between Insert and Overtype modes. When entering text, Insert mode adds text, and Overtype mode will type over existing text.
- Number Keypad: Allows typing numbers when Num Lock (15) is on.
- Num Lock: Turns on or off typing of numbers in the Number Keypad. When on, the Num Lock light (8) will be lit.
- Shift: Used in combination with other keys to capitalize letters (Shift with 'A' types capital 'A') and also to access the alternate characters printed on some keys (Shift with '2' types '@').
- Tab: Used for indenting - inserts a fixed number of spaces.

Shift Key

The shift key is used in combination with other keys to make capital letters and to type symbols on the keyboard. Meaning, you hold down the shift key at the same time you type another key. For example, to type a capital 'G', press and hold down the shift key with one finger, then press the 'G' key once with another finger.

You may notice some keys have more than one symbol on them - an upper symbol and a lower symbol. When the key is pressed, the lower symbol is what is typed. To get the upper symbol to be typed, you will need to hold down the shift key and then press the key with the symbol once. For example, to type an exclamation point, press and hold down the shift key with one finger, then press the '1' key once with another finger.

Backspace Key

When you type, it is not uncommon to make mistakes in spelling. Thankfully there is a button to help you erase mistakes. When you make a mistake, you can press the backspace key. The backspace button is located up and to the right. When you press the backspace key, it will erase one letter back. Pressing Backspace will also remove lines you created by pressing the enter key. If you notice a mistake in the beginning, simply use the arrow keys to move the cursor to where you want to begin erasing, and then press the backspace key.

The Touchscreen

Using the Touchscreen

Your computer has a touchscreen, meaning you can use your finger or the stylus that came with your computer to touch it. The stylus is the small pointing device that looks like a pen. Using the touch screen is very similar to using the mouse, but rather than using the mouse to control the pointer on the screen, you just tap the screen with your finger. If you've never used a mouse, you may find it easier to use the touchscreen. For example, if I want to see the Weather, simply press the Weather button with your finger to GO to the Weather application. You can also use the stylus that came with your computer to touch the screen.

Online User Manual

The Online User Manual is a window that opens when you press the Help button, located at the top right corner of your computer screen. It contains all the information in this User Manual. Clicking Help will display the chapter related to what you are currently doing. To show or hide the table of contents, press the Index button to see what chapters we have available. To read a chapter, simply press on a chapter name and the computer will GO to that chapter. You can watch videos by pressing the Video button at the top of the window. To get back to the written word, press the *Text* button at the top of the window. Also at the top of the Help window is a droplist that shows you the different sections in the chapter that you are currently reading. Simply press the down arrow to view the list, then, press on a section name to go to it. If the list is long, you can use your scroll bar skills to move up and down in the list. If you have a printer attached to your computer, you can easily print out a chapter to read later by pressing the print button located at the top of this window:

Overview

Understanding the Screen Layout

Your computer screen is divided into three sections:

- Title Area: this is the area across the top of the screen. It will always remain present. It contains the *Date* and *Time*, the *Network Connection* icon, and the *Volume*, *Help* and *Settings* buttons.
- Application Buttons: these are the blue buttons along the left side of the screen. These buttons will always remain present. Clicking on an *application button* will go to that application.

- Application Area: this is the large rectangular area to the right of the blue application buttons. This area changes based on what blue button you click. For example, if you click the *Weather* button, the application Area will show you information about the weather. Similarly, if you click the *News* button, the application area will show you the news headlines.

Title Area

Date and Time

The current date and time are always displayed at the top of the screen. To change your time zone, click Settings, then click System Settings and select your time zone from the droplist.

NOTE: Your computer gets its date and time from the internet. If you are not connected to the internet, your date and time may be off. Once you connect to the internet, your date and time will be corrected. It may take a few minutes for the time to update once you are connected to the internet.

If you are not connected to the internet and want to set the correct time, please do the following:

- Click Home
- Click Settings
- Click System Settings
- Click Set Time
- Enter the correct time
- Click OK

 Network Connection Icon

This icon reflects your network connection status. If all four bars are blue, then you have a strong connection. Each bar that is not blue represents a weaker connection.

TECH TIP: It is a good idea to keep track of this icon, as many of the computer's functions require a strong internet connection.

 Volume Control

To adjust the master volume on your computer, click the *Volume* button and then use your finger or mouse to drag the volume slider bar up and down to increase or decrease the volume.

 Screen Magnifier

After clicking the Screen Magnifier button, a rectangular box will appear around your cursor. This box magnifies whatever it is placed over top of, comparable to using a magnifying glass. You can use this to help read your computer screen easier as well as make selecting links and highlighting text easier. While the Screen Magnifier is active, your cursor will still function normally. To deactivate the Screen Magnifier, click the Magnifier. Alternatively, pressing the **Esc** key on your keyboard will also deactivate the Screen Magnifier.

 Help

This button opens up the **Help** page for the application or feature that you are viewing. The **Help** files are your built-in **User Manual** and feature both Text and Video Tutorials. To learn more about the **Help** files and the benefits of using them, follow these instructions:

1. Click Index, located at the bottom of this window
2. Click *Getting Help*, located in the left-hand panel under the heading **Your Computer**.

When you are done using the Help files, click the red *Close* button located at the bottom of this window.

Settings Button

The *Settings* button allows you to manage simple settings that control the operation of your computer. You may configure your personal user profile in the settings area, as well as set up your email and other accounts.

Application buttons

The application buttons are always visible on the left-hand side of the screen. Simply click an application button to go to that application. Switching between applications is easy too - just click the application button for the application you want to use next!

Home	Brings you to the Home screen, a familiar place to begin.
Video Chat	Allows you to make video and audio calls to all of your Skype contacts. For more information on Video Chat, click the *Video Chat* application button, then click *Help*.
Email	Allows you to read, send and manage all your email messages. For more information on Email, click the *Email* application button, then click *Help*
Photos	Allows you to view photos stored on your computer, as well as photos from your Facebook friends. You can also upload new photos and arrange your photos in albums. This is also where you select the photos for your *Favorites* album. For more information on Photos, click the *Photos* application button, and then click *Help*.
Calendar	Allows you to view the calendar by day, week or month. You can schedule events for birthdays, appointments or holidays and set reminders. For more information on the calendar, click the *Calendar* application button, then click *Help*.
Contacts	Allows you to store and manage your contacts. You can enter addresses, phone numbers, email addresses, birthdays and more. For more information on Contacts, click the *Contacts* application button, and then click *Help*.

Weather Allows you to view a five day forecast and a Doppler map and get weather for different zip codes. For more information on Weather, click the Weather application button, then click Help.

News Allows you to view current headlines from a variety of categories and to change your news source. For more information on News, click the *News* application button, then click *Help*.

Web Allows you to view web pages and bookmark your favorite sites and provides you with a list of quick links to popular sites like Google, eBay, YouTube and more! For more information on the web browser, click the *Web* application button, then click *Help*.

Games Allows you to play games. Your computer comes preloaded with several games, such as Solitaire, Blackjack and FreeCell. For more information on Games, click the *Games* application button, and then click *Help*.

More Here you will find more features and tools, such as a timer, a calculator, conversion tools, a word processor and more. For more information, click the *More...* application button, then click *Help*.

Magnification

These magnification buttons allow you to increase or decrease the size of the text. They are available when you are reading email or news, or are browsing the *Web*. Simply click the button with the '+' to increase magnification, or, alternately, click the '-' button to decrease magnification.

NOTE: Scroll bars will also be magnified. This allows you to click them more easily. Also, some content on web pages may not appear when magnification is used. This is due to the design of the web page, not your computer.

Home

The Home screen, as its name implies, is a familiar place to begin. It will always be displayed when you turn on your computer, and will provide you with a quick overview of what's happening in your world.

From the Home screen, you will be able to log in to your account, access all of the features of your computer and view important notices.

To get to the Home Screen, click the Home button.
When you click the Home button, the application area will show a Photo Viewer, a Notices board and several Widgets.

Notices	The Notices board displays events that need your attention. Types of notifications include Software Updates, new email messages, new contact information, missed video chat calls, or calendar event reminders. Clicking a notice will allow you to take action on the notice. For example, clicking on a notice that informs you of new emails will take you to your email inbox. Similarly, clicking a new Software Update notice will prompt you to restart your computer to complete the update.
Photo Viewer	The photo viewer displays photos that are saved in your Favorites album. The viewer will rotate through these photos to create a pleasing display.
Widgets	The Home screen contains small information boxes, called widgets. These widgets give you a brief overview of information. Clicking a widget will give you more detailed information.
News Widget	Shows a sub-set of the top stories from your choice of new sources. Click a headline in the News widget to see the full story.
Weather Widget	Shows a concise view of current and pending weather conditions. Click the Weather widget to see a live Doppler radar map of the weather in your area as well as a full 5-day forecast.
Quotes & Trivia Widget	Shows random quotes or trivia questions for your enjoyment. A new quote or trivia question will be shown each time you return to the home page. You can also click the Quotes or Trivia tab to bring up a new quote or trivia question.

Logging In

Login Button

If you have created user accounts on your computer, when you turn on the computer you will see a green Login button near the top right corner of the screen. If you have not created any user accounts, then you will not see the Login button.

To login, do one of the following:

- If only one user account has been created, and you **do not have** a password defined for this account, simply click Login.
- If only one user account has been created, and you do have a password defined for this account, enter your password, and then click Login.

- If multiple user accounts have been configured, select your username from the droplist, enter your password (if one is defined), and then click Login. If you are the Primary user, there will be a star next to your username that will always be displayed at the top of the droplist.

Guest Mode

When you have created user accounts and have not logged in yet, the computer is in **Guest Mode**. You may still use the computer in **Guest Mode**, but with limited functionality. **Guest Mode** adds a level of privacy and security to your computer that is useful when you would like guests or children to be able to use your computer, but not be able to see your email or your contacts or other private information.

Features that can be used in **Guest Mode**:

- Home - access to the **Home** screen
- Weather
- News
- Web - surfing the internet
- Games
- More... - helpful tools

Features that are disabled in **Guest Mode**:

- Video Chat
- Email
- Photos
- Calendar
- Contacts

 Video Chat

Video Chat allows you to send and receive free video and audio calls to friends and family across the globe.

To go use the Video Chat application, click the Video Chat button.

In order to make Video Chat calls, the following must be true:

- Your computer must be connected to the Internet.
- You must have a Skype™* account.
- Your computer must be configured with your Skype account and successfully logged into your Skype account.

Additionally, for the person you want to call, the following must be true:

- They must have a Skype account.

- They must have Skype software installed and active on their computer.
- They must be one of your Skype contacts (this means your Skype accounts are linked together).

* Skype is a technology that allows you to make free video and audio calls through your computer.

Internet Connection

To determine if you are connected to the Internet, look for the connection icon: 📶 at the top of your screen. It should display at least one blue bar. If there are no blue bars, then you are not connected to the internet. Click the connection icon to manage your network connection.

Configure Video Chat

In order to use Video Chat, you will need to enter your Skype account username and password into your computer and log in to Skype. This information is entered in the **Video Chat Settings** page. This page will also allow you to create a new Skype account if you don't have one. Follow these instructions to get to the **Video Chat Settings** page and enter your Skype account:

1. Click **Video Chat**
2. Click **Settings**. Alternatively, you can click on the video window instead.

See the chapter on Video Chat Settings to get more information on filling out the fields or creating a new Skype account.

Import Contacts

If you already have a Skype account with existing contacts, you will be able to import these contacts into your computer. Shortly after you configure the computer with your Skype account, a message will appear in the **Notices** section of the **Home** screen indicating you have Skype contacts to import. To import these contacts, simply click the message. This will open a window listing your contacts. To import a contact to your **Address Book**, click the **Import** button next to the contact's name. You'll need to do this for each contact you want to import. For any contacts you don't want to keep, click the **Dismiss** button next to that contact's name.

Skype Contacts

Understanding Skype Contacts

A Skype Contact is a person whose Skype account is linked to your Skype account so that you can communicate each other using the **Video Chat** application. In order to use **Video Chat** you will need to create Skype contact relationships with the people you want to call.

Understanding Skype Contact Requests

In order to create a Skype contact, a Skype contact request must be sent - either from you to the person with whom you wish to Video Chat or from them to you. When a Skype contact request is received, it must then be confirmed to complete the process.

Send a Skype Contact Request

To initiate a Skype contact request, follow these instructions:

If this is an existing contact in your Address Book...
1. Click Video Chat.
2. Click the name of the contact in the Address Book on the right of your screen.
3. Click Send Contact Request. A pop-up window will appear.
4. Click Find to generate a list of possible matches.
5. If you find the person, click their name and then click Add User Name. This generates a Skype contact request to that person. Once they accept this contact request, your accounts will be linked.
6. If you cannot find the person - or are unsure - click Email for Video Chat Name. This sends them an email with your Skype username requesting that they add you as a Skype contact. When they add you as a Skype contact, you will receive a Skype contact request. Follow the instructions in the Receive a Skype Contact Request section to accept the request and link your accounts.

If this is a new contact...
1. Click Video Chat.
2. Click Add Contact.
3. Enter the contact's first and last names and click OK.
4. Click Find to generate a list of possible matches.
5. **If you find the person,** click their name and then click Add User Name. This generates a Skype contact request to that person. Once they accept this contact request, your accounts will be linked.
6. **If you cannot find the person** - or are unsure - click Close, then click Contacts. Add their email address to your address book and follow the instructions for an existing contact listed above.

When your Skype accounts are linked, you will see the Skype username and a Skype status icon appear in the Address Book for that person.

Receive a Skype Contact Request

If a person sends a Skype contact request to you, you will see a notice on your Home screen indicating you have a new contact. Clicking the notice will take you to the Contacts application where you can add the Skype contact.

Using Video Chat

Make a Video Call

You will only be able to make video calls to contacts that are online. To make a video call, follow these instructions:

1. Click **Video Chat**.
2. Click the name of your Skype contact in the **Address Book**. Their name will be highlighted, and their name, Skype name, status, and four buttons will appear in the video window. The four buttons are: **Video Call**, **Audio Only**, **Edit**, and **Remove**.
3. Click **Video Call**. (Click **Audio Call** if you want to make a call without video.)

This will initiate the video call. When the person you are calling answers, you will see them in the center of the screen. You will also see yourself in a video inset at the bottom.

End a Video Call

Click **End Call** to end the current video or audio call.

Adjust the Call Volume

You can adjust the incoming volume of your video chat call by dragging the volume slider to the right to increase volume and to the left to decrease volume.

Mute/Unmute a Call

You can mute the outgoing sound during a call by clicking the **Mute** button. The person you are speaking with via video chat will no longer be able to hear you. When the call is muted, the **Mute** button will change to an **Unmute** button. Clicking **Unmute** will allow the person you are speaking with via video chat to hear you again.

Missed Calls

It is a good idea to plan your video calls. If your Skype contact is not online or not available to accept your call, they will miss the call. Similarly, if you are not available to accept a call, it will be missed. The good news is that you may easily view your missed calls. To view your missed calls, do the following:

1. Click **Video Chat**.
2. Click **Missed Calls**.

After you view your missed calls, you can remove them by selecting them and clicking **Remove**, which is located to the right of the **Missed Calls** button.

You will see the date, time, and name of the contact for any missed calls. Clicking the name of the caller will set up a video call to that contact.

Skype Status Icons

When browsing through your **Address Book** while in the **Video Chat** application, you will notice a small icon below the name of each of your contacts. These are **status icons**. Status icons are used to indicate the availability of your contact. You will only be able to make video calls to contacts that are online.

Below is a list of the status icons.

🟢 The contact is online.

🕐 The contact is online, but stepped away from their computer.

🕐 The contact is online, but has been away from their computer for a period of time.

⬛ The contact is online, but has indicated that they are busy.

✴️ The contact is not online.

📧 Email Inbox

Email stands for "electronic mail". In order to use email, you will need to have an email account and a working internet connection.

It is a good idea to keep your inbox organized. Just like your regular mail, you'll want to read your emails daily and delete unwanted or old emails (similar to throwing away junk mail). You can also organize your inbox by moving important emails to folders.

To view the email inbox, click the Email button.

Understanding the Inbox

The inbox is a list of all the email messages you have received. Email is sorted by date, with the most recent email at the top of the list. For each email in the list, you will see the subject whether or not it has attachments, the sender and the date it was sent.

Subject
The subject of the email is displayed in this column.

Attachments
📎 If you see this icon in the column, it means that the email message has one or more attachments.

Replied
↩️ If you see this icon in the column, it means that you replied to this email at some point. It's a way to help you keep track of the email that you have replied to.

From
The sender of the email is displayed in this column.

Date
This column displays the date the email was sent.

Checkbox

The checkbox is used to select several emails at once. This is convenient for moving or deleting several emails.

Creating, Reading, and Forwarding an Email

Create an Email

To create an email, click the Email button, and then click **Compose Email**. This will open a new email message. Click **Help** when viewing the new email message to get more information on how to address, compose and send your email.

Read an Email

To read an email, just click the Email button and then click the subject line of the email! This will open the email so you can read it.

Forward an Email

You may forward an email you have received to one or more people in your contacts list. To forward an email, click the email you wish to forward. Clicking on the subject line of the email will open it as if you wanted to read it. Then click the **Forward** button on the right-hand side of the screen. The Compose Email screen will be brought up so that you can fill in the **To:** and **CC:** fields. You can also attach files and type a message in the body. When you are satisfied with your message, press the Send button.

Managing Email

Delete Email

You can organize your emails by deleting unwanted or old emails. Click the check box next to the email(s) you want to delete and then click Delete. You will be asked to confirm your decision.

Move Email

You can organize your emails by moving them to different folders. Click the check box next to the email(s) you want to move and then click Move... You will then be prompted to select the destination folder. Click the destination folder, and then click Ok.

Find an Email

Click the **Find...** button to initiate a search for emails based on a word or a phrase in the email. To find email, follow these instructions:

1. Click **Find...**
2. Enter the word(s) to search for
3. Click Ok
4. A list of emails containing the search word(s) will appear.
5. To cancel the search and see your inbox again, click **Clear Search**.

Refresh Mail

The computer checks for new email automatically every 10 minutes. Clicking "Refresh Mail" makes this happen immediately.

Folders

Folders are used to organize and store your emails. You can move important emails into folders to store them for later reference. To view a different folder, click the folder name. The most commonly used folders are:

Inbox Folder

All new emails go into your inbox. Click **Inbox** to view emails in the Inbox.

Sent Folder

All sent emails go into your sent folder. Click **Sent** to view emails in the Sent folder.

Drafts Folder

Emails that you are working on and save for later will be saved to this folder. Click **Drafts** to view emails that have been saved to the Drafts folder.

Trash

When you delete an email, it is moved to the **Trash** folder. An email that has been deleted will remain in the **Trash** folder for 10 days before it is permanently deleted. To remove an email from the **Trash** folder, perform the following steps:

1. Click Trash
2. Find the email(s) that you want to remove from the Trash
3. Click the checkbox(es) to the left of the email(s)
4. Click **Move...**
5. Click the destination folder
6. Click Ok

Other Folders

In addition to the commonly used folders, you can create other folders to manage your emails. To create new folders, simply click **Email**, and then click **Settings**. Please see the **Managing Folders** section below for more detailed information on managing folders. If you configure your computer with an existing email account that has folders, those folders will be imported.

Managing Folders

To create, rename or delete folders, simply click **Email**, click **Settings**, and then click **Folders**. On this page, you will see a list of your existing folders. If you have more folders than are visible on one page, a scroll bar will appear to the right to allow you to scroll through your folder list.

NOTE: Folders will be synchronized between the computer and the mail server only for email accounts configured with IMAP.

To create a folder, simply click **Add**, enter a name for your new folder, and then click **OK**.

To rename a folder, click the checkbox to the left of the folder name and then click **Rename**. Enter a new name for the folder and then click **OK**.

To delete a folder, click the checkbox to the left of the folder name and then click **Remove**. If you click **OK**, this will remove the folder and all the emails in it.

Composing an Email

This screen allows you to compose, address and send your email message, as well as add or remove attachments.

To compose email:
- **Click the Email button**
- **Click the Compose Email button**

Email Message Components

Emails are composed of two parts: the header area and the message body.

The header is the gray area at the top of the email. When creating new email, this is where you address your email and add or remove attachments. When reading emails that have already been sent or received, this area also includes a timestamp (date and time) for when the email was sent, plus the ability to view attachments.

The message body is the large white area below the header. This is the actual email message. To begin, click in the message body, a blinking cursor to appear. The cursor is the insertion point where typing will begin - it's like putting a pencil down on paper. Once you have typed your email and are ready to send it, click **Send**. When the recipient responds to you, the email body will contain their response. The body keeps all the communication in one place, so you can read through the conversation.

To:

This field lists the recipients of the email. Simply click in the white box to the right of the **To:** button and begin typing the email addresses of the email recipients. If you are typing more than one email address, separate the addresses with a semicolon: ';'.

If some of the email recipients have their email addresses recorded in your **Contacts**, you can click the **To:** button, and get them directly from the Address Book. If you select a contact that has more than one email in your address book, the email will be sent to the address listed as **Email 1** in their Contact information.

CC:

"CC" stands for "Carbon Copy", a term used in letter writing. This field is similar to the To: field in that you can specify recipients who will receive a copy of the email. It is mostly used for organizational purposes.

To carbon copy recipients, click the CC: button to add recipients from your Address Book, or type the email addresses into the text field to the right of the CC: button. Use a semicolon to separate multiple email addresses.

Attach File...

Click this button to add photos, documents or other files as attachments. When you click Attach File, you will be presented with a series of windows that will guide you through selecting what files you want to send along with the email.

If you want to remove a file that you have attached to an email - or are forwarding an email and want to remove one or more of the attachments - click Attach File.... A popup window will open displaying all of the files that are currently attached to your email. To remove a file, simply click Remove. When you are satisfied with your attachments, click Close.

Subject

Click in the field to the right of the word Subject: to enter a subject for the email. This gives the recipient an idea of what the email is about. An example of a subject might be "Want to meet for lunch?"

Send the Email

When you have completed your email and wish to send it, simply click Send. If you decide not to send the email, click Cancel and you will be prompted to confirm the cancellation.

Spell Check

When you are composing an email, you might notice that occasionally words are underlined with a jagged red line. This means that these words may be misspelled. You can right-click the underlined word to see possible corrections. Please be aware that the red line does not necessarily mean that a word IS misspelled but rather that it is not recognized by the computer. A common example of this is a person's last name.

Email Functions

 Zoom In/Out

Clicking these buttons will enlarge or decrease the size of the text in the email message body to make it easier to read.

Print

If you have a printer plugged into your computer, clicking the **Print** button will open a **Print Request** popup. This popup lets you choose a printer to use, the orientation of your paper, and the number of copies you wish to print. When you have selected your options, click the green **Print** button to print your email.

Send

Clicking the Send button sends the current email to the recipients listed in the To: and CC: fields.

Save Draft

Clicking the **Save Draft** button saves the current email in the Drafts folder. You may wish to do this if you don't have the email address of the person you wish to send the email to or just as a precaution. The draft will stay in the Drafts folder until the email is sent.

Delete

Clicking the **Delete** button cancels the new email and returns to the *Inbox*. You will be asked to confirm leaving since this will delete the current email in progress.

Keyboard Controls

Functions like **Cut**, **Copy**, and **Paste** can be utilized by using a combination of keystrokes. To Cut or Copy, simply highlight the text you wish to duplicate. Then:

- Simultaneously press ctrl, located in the bottom left corner of your keyboard, and "C", if you want to **Copy** the text.
- Simultaneously press ctrl and "X", if you want to **Cut** the text.

To **Paste** text that you have copied or cut, simply click where you would like to place the text, then simultaneously press ctrl and "V".

NOTE: Keyboard Controls can only be utilized by using a real keyboard; the on-screen keyboard will not work.

Reading an Email

This screen shows an individual email message.

To read email:
- **Click the Email button**
- **Click the words of the Subject of an individual email**

Email Message

Message Header

The message header is the gray area at the top the email. It represents the "envelope" of the email. The header displays the timestamp (date and time) the email was received/sent, the subject of the email, the sender/receiver and any attachments that may have been sent with the email.

Message Body

The message body is the white area below the header. This is the actual email message. This is where the email conversation is displayed. Use the blue scroll bars to scroll through the conversation.

If the body contains any web links, clicking on a link will open a popup window displaying the website. Click the Close button to close the popup window.

You can use the zoom buttons (see below) to increase or decrease the size of the text displayed in the message body.

Email Attachments

Email attachments are files that are sent with the email. There are many kinds of attachments. Examples of attachments are images, documents, contact information, spreadsheets, videos, music, or calendar events.

Currently, you may view images, documents (Word compatible documents or PDF files), contact information, videos, music, and calendar events. You are able to save unsupported file types; however, you will not be able to view these files at this time. You will be able to view these files in the near future.

Viewing Email Attachments

You can view attachments directly from the email by clicking View Attachments. The attachment will open in a viewing window. Click the Close button to close the attachment window.

If the attachment you are viewing is a **video** or **audio** file, you can view / listen to that file directly in the view attachments popup.

If the attachment you received is **Contact Information**, then it will automatically be saved and added to your contact list. If the contact is already in your contact list, then any information that is new will be added to that contact; however if there is information that would overwrite previously saved information, then you must view the attachment and save it manually to confirm the change. For example, Let's say John Doe is in your address book with just his name, email address, and phone number, so he sends you his contact information by email that includes his current home address, but a new phone number. When you open his email, you will see a dialog box that says "Contact information saved" and his home address will be added to your address book; however in order to save his new phone number you must view the attachment and click Save.

Saving Email Attachments

When you view the attachments, you will also have the option to save them to your computer. To save an attachment, click the Save button. If you are saving a document, the File Manager will open where you can select a destination folder. If you are saving an image, you will be prompted to save it to one of your albums.

To view your saved documents, use the File Manager, accessible by clicking the More button. To view your saved images, click the Photos to view your albums.

Email Message Functions

Zoom In/Out

Clicking these buttons will increase or decrease the size of the message, making it easier to read.

CC:

Clicking this button allows you to add the email address of anyone who was Carbon Copied in the message to your address book by either creating a new contact or updating an existing contact. This button will only appear if at least one person was **Carbon Copied** in the message.

TO:

Clicking this button allows you to add the email address of a person receiving this email to your address book by either creating a new contact or updating an existing contact. This button will only appear if the message was sent to another email via the To: message field.

From:

Clicking this button allows you to add the sender's email address to your address book by either creating a new contact or updating an existing contact.

Reply/Reply All:

Clicking this button will bring up a dialog box asking if you want to **Reply to Sender** or **All recipients**. Replying to Sender will allow you to write an email to the person who wrote the email to which you are replying, while Replying to All recipients will send it to everyone who received the original email as well as the sender.

TECH TIP: If you want to reply to some but not all of the recipients then:

1. Click the Reply.
2. Click All.
3. When your reply email opens, erase the email addresses of those that you do not wish to send the message to.

Forward:

Forwarding an email sends an email you have received to one or more people in your contacts list. To forward an email, click the Forward button on the right-hand side of the screen. The Compose Email screen will be brought up so that you can fill in the To: and CC: fields. You can also attach files and type a message in the body. When you are satisfied with your message, press send.

Delete

Deletes the current email. You will be asked to confirm this decision.

Move...

Moves the current email to a different folder. This is very helpful when organizing your emails. A pop-up window will appear asking you to select Inbox, Sent, Folder 1, or Folder 2.

Print

If you have a printer connected to your computer and turned on, click **Print** to print the current email.

Email Navigation Functions

Next   Shows the next email in the list.

Previous   Shows the previous email in the list.

Back to Inbox   Returns you to the **Inbox**. This button reflects your current folder. For example, if you are viewing sent items, this button will change to **Back to Sent Mail**.

Returns you to the **Inbox**. This button reflects your current folder. For example, if you are viewing sent items, this button will change to **Back to Sent Mail**.

Photos

Photos lets you easily view, manage and upload digital photos. To use the Facebook feature, you will need a working internet connection, a Facebook account and have your computer configured with that account.

To view photos, click the Photos button.

The Photos application lets you store and view digital photos on your computer and organize them into albums. You can upload photos to your computer directly from your camera, camera card or external storage device.

If you have a Facebook account, and your computer is configured to use the account, your friends' photos will be automatically loaded onto your computer as well. Additionally, images you receive as attachments in email can be saved into your albums.

Albums

The Photos application uses the concept of albums to group your photos. Just like a real photo album, you can add or remove photos from these albums. Albums that contain photos which are stored on the computer display with a blue binding. If you're logged-in to your Facebook account, your friends' photos will display with a brown binder to differentiate them from your local albums.

Favorites album

Photos stored in the Favorites album are used to create the photo slideshow that you see on the **Home** screen. You can easily move photos from other albums to your Favorites album to create a visually pleasing display.

It's easy to add a photo to the Favorites album. While viewing the photo you would like to add, click **Add to Album...**, click the **Favorites** album, and then click **OK**. You can even move photos from your friends' Facebook albums into the Favorites folder!

My Albums

The My Albums folder contains all of the albums that you create on your computer and any albums you may have created in your Facebook account. The albums on your computer will display with a **blue** binder; Facebook albums with a brown binder.

Facebook albums

Your computer loads friends' and family's photo albums right from Facebook. These albums will display with a **brown** colored binder. The album cover will display the photo your friend has as their profile picture on Facebook.

If any of your friends add new photos to their albums, you will see a notification icon on the **Photos** button and also on the album in which your friends has added new photo(s).

Creating an album

To get started creating albums, click the My Albums folder and then click Create New Album. Enter a name and click OK. The album will appear in the My Albums folder. You can then begin adding photos to this new album.

Clear Notifications

The notification icon will appear when your friends have added new photos to their Facebook albums. Clicking this button will remove all notification icons. You can turn off the notification light from an album by simply clicking the album and viewing the new photo(s)

Uploading Photos

Loading photos is easy! Simply attach a device or insert a card and follow the instructions below for copying/moving photos.

Attaching a USB Device

A USB device may be a camera, an external hard drive, or a USB stick. Attach the USB cable into your camera or external storage device. Then, plug the other end of the USB connector into one of the USB ports in the computer. To locate USB ports, refer to the **Quick Start Guide** that came with the computer.

Inserting a Camera Card

Insert your camera card into the 4-in-1 card reader port, the rectangular slit located on the left side of the computer.

After your device is plugged into the computer, click More then click File Manager. When the card appears on the From side, the photos are ready to be copied or moved to your computer. For instructions on using the File Manager, click More. click File Manager and then click Help.

 My Albums

My Albums contains all the albums you create on your computer and, if you have any, your personal Facebook albums. Here you can create new albums, edit existing albums or delete unwanted albums.

To view an album:
- **Click the Photos button**
- **Click the album group titled, My Albums**

Create an Album

Creating an album is quick and easy. To create a new album, click the Create New Album button, type in a name for the album, and then click Ok. Once you've created a new local album, you can begin moving or copying photos into it by uploading photos from your camera or external device or by moving photos from other albums. You can even copy photos from your friends' Facebook albums into any locally created (blue) album!

Edit Album Information

Once you've created a new album, you can edit the album information. Simply click the Edit button at the bottom of the album, edit the fields you wish to change and click Save.

NOTE: You cannot delete, edit or add to any Facebook photo albums (brown albums) that appear in the My Albums folder. These albums can only be edited in Facebook.

 Facebook Albums

Facebook albums are albums that are imported to the Photos application from your Facebook account. These albums are identified by their brown binder, whereas albums created and stored on your computer have a blue binder.

Your computer will import all the albums that your Facebook friends have posted to Facebook and shared with you. Albums or photos that they mark as private - or do not share with you - will not be imported into your computer. If you are not seeing a Facebook friend's albums or photos, have them check the permissions on that album/photo to make sure it is shared with you.

An interesting differentiation between Facebook (brown) and local (blue) albums is that Facebook albums are not stored on your computer. They are temporarily imported for viewing only. This means that you cannot delete or edit these photos.

If you like a particular photo and want to move it to your computer to view on the Home page in the rotating photo display, you can copy a Facebook photo to your computer using: while viewing the individual photo, simply click the Add to Album... button and copy it to your Favorites album. In fact, you can move it to any local album you want. This will allow you to edit the photo, or use it for an album cover by clicking the Make Album Cover button.

 # Viewing and Managing Photos

Viewing and managing the photos in your albums is simple and easy. You can switch the order of photos; choose a particular photo to be used as an album cover, move photos to other albums, print and much more!

To view and manage photos:
- **Click the Photos button**
- **Click the album group titled, My Albums**
- **Click an album**

Navigation Functions

Thumbnail View

Thumbnail view allows you to get a better idea of what, and how many, photos are in an album. It creates smaller representations of each photo so that you can easily find the photo you are looking for. Simply click the thumbnail of a photo to view it larger.

If you would like to change the order of the photos, click the **Organize** button that appears in the top right corner of the thumbnail view. Click a photo and use the arrow buttons to move the photo to the desired location. When you are happy with the order of the photos in the album, click Done.

Slideshow

Slideshow is a great way to show friends and family photos in your albums. Clicking the Slideshow button brings you to a picture viewer that will cycle through all the photos in the current album with a 10 second delay between each photo. Click **Next** to move to the next photo instead of waiting for the delay. Click **Previous** to get back to a photo you have passed. Clicking **Pause** will stop the slideshow. Once you are done viewing a slideshow, you can click Close to return to the last screen you were on.

Previous / Next

Use the ◀ and ▶ buttons to navigate through your photos. The ◀ button, located to the left of the current photo, will take you to the **previous** photo in the album. The ▶ button, located to the right of the current photo, will take you to the **next** photo in the album.

Photo Function Buttons

Share

Clicking the **Share** button will automatically attach the current photo to a blank email so that you can send it to friends and family.

Add to Album...

You can copy or move photos to any one of the local (blue) albums that you've created, including the **Favorites*** album. Simply use the Previous and Next buttons to find the photo that you would like copy or move and click Add to Album.... Finally, choose a destination folder for the photo you are moving/copying.

* Photos added to your **Favorites** album will appear in the Digital Photo Frame on the **Home** screen.

Make Album Cover

The **Make Album Cover** option is only available for photos in your local (blue) albums. This feature allows you to select a photo to use as the album cover for the current album. While viewing a photo you want as the album cover, select **Make Album Cover**.

Delete

The Delete option is only available for photos in your local (blue) albums. It allows you to remove any unwanted photos or duplicates from the current album. While viewing a photo you want to delete, select **Delete**.

Edit Photo

The **Edit Photo** button is only available for photos in your local (blue) albums. While viewing a photo you want to edit, click Edit Photo. A variety of editing options will appear on the right for you to choose from. Select the editing option you would like to perform on the photo, and when you are happy with the newly edited photo, click Done.

TECH TIP: If you are just learning how to edit photos or are experimenting with the tools, you may want to create duplicates of the photos you are editing so you will not have to worry if you make a mistake. To do this, follow these instructions:

1. Go to **My Albums**.
2. Click **Create New Album** and name the album.
3. Go through your albums and/or your friends albums and find the photos you want to edit.
4. When you find a photo you would like to edit, Click Add to Album... and select the album you just created.
5. After you have finished looking for photos to edit, go to the album that you placed the photos in.
6. Start editing and have fun.

7. If you like how it looks when you have finished editing, you can add it to any album you would like or leave it in that album.

Rotate

This option allows you to rotate the photo using the following options:

- **Rotate Left** - Turns the photo 90 degrees counter-clockwise.
- **Rotate Right** - Turns the photo 90 degrees clockwise.
- **Flip Horizontal** - Flips the photo from Right to Left. For example, if the photo you were editing was ◀ and you click **Flip Horizontal** then the photo would now be ▶.
- **Flip Vertical** – Flips the photo top to bottom. If the photo you were editing was ▲ and you click **Flip Vertical** then the photo would now be ▼.
- **Free Rotate** - This button allows you to rotate your photo yourself. Clicking this button will put boxes in the four corners of your photo and a red dot at the center. Click one of the boxes and, without lifting your finger, move the box in the direction you wish to turn the photo. Lift your finger when it is oriented to your liking.
- **Undo** - This button allows you to undo the last change made to your photo. There is no limit to the amount of times you can use this button.
- **Done** - When you are satisfied with your photo, clicking done will save all of your changes and take you back to the Edit Photo page. Do not click this button unless you are absolutely sure that you are satisfied with how your photo looks because you will not be able to undo the changes.

Crop

This option allows you to cut off sections of your photo. For instance, let's say that your family took a picture in front of a funny carnival background, but when you looked at the photo, you noticed that the area above the background is visible. With the crop tool, you can remove that section of the photo so that the area above the carnival background isn't visible.

Horizon

This option lets you rotate your photo so that line you set as the horizon will be perfectly horizontal.

Red Eye

This option allows you to remove certain amounts of the color red from either an entire picture or specific areas. The main use for this option is to remove the red eyes that occasionally show up in photos. The **Red-eye threshold** slider determines how much red is removed - slide this back and forth to get the effect you want. The **Choose eyes** button lets you focus the red-eye remover over specific areas. This is useful if the red removal seems to remove red from the wrong areas of the photo. Simply click the **Choose eyes** button and click the eyes in the photo. You can remove an area by clicking on it a second time. The **Search zone size** slider makes the eye zones smaller or larger.

Contrast

This option lets you adjust how your photo looks using a variety of options.

- **Brightness** - This slider will make your photo darker or brighter.
- **Contrast** - This slider will determine the difference between the light and dark colors in the photo. When the slider is moved to the right, the difference between the dark and light colors increase, but when the slider is moved left, the difference between the light and dark colors will decrease and become more similar.
- **Saturation** - This slider allows you to change the vibrancy of the colors in your photo. The more the slider is moved to the right, the more vivid the photo will be, and the more the slider is moved to the left the more washed out the photo becomes.
- **Color Balance** - This slide allows you to adjust or change the color of the photo. This tool can be used to slightly modify a photo to your liking or to change the photo drastically to be artistic or zany.

Printing Photos

To print one or more photos in the current album, follow these instructions:

1. Click **Print**.
2. Click **Select Photos**.
3. Click the photo(s) you would like to print. You can click the photo(s) again to deselect.
4. Click Ok.
5. Click a printing option (see Printing Options below). The default printing option of "1 per page 8x10" will be selected. If this is what you want, simply click **Print**. To print several smaller copies of the photo on one page, click a different printing option, then click **Print**.

Printing Options

Sizes are shown in inches. The following sizes are available:

- 5 x 7 - will print one photo per page.
- 4 x 6 - will print two photos per page.
- 3 x 5 - will print four photos per page.
- 2.2 x 3.5 - will print photos six per page.
- 2.5 x 3 - will print eight photos per page.

NOTE: If you select an option that will print several photos per page, but you only choose one photo to print, only one photo will be printed in the smaller size.

Thumbnail View

This view allows you to see all of the photos in your current album. From this screen you can see how many photos are in the album, view a specific photo, and organize your photos.

To view thumbnails
- **Click the Photos button**
- **Click the album group titled, My Albums**
- **Click an album**

Navigation

This view allows you to quickly navigate to a particular photo. Simply find the photo and click it to view that photo.

Organize

You can organize the photos in your albums and your friends' albums to your liking. To organize your albums, follow these instructions:

1. Click **Organize**, located in the top right corner.
2. Click the photo you want to move.
3. Use the arrow buttons, located in the top right corner, to move the photo to where you want it.
4. The ▲ and ▼ buttons moves the photo vertically by one row.
5. The ◄ and ► buttons move the photo horizontally by one column.
6. When you are satisfied with how the photos are arranged, click **Done** - located to the right of the arrow buttons.

Back to Photo View

This button will bring you back to photo view at the first photo in your album.

Calendar

This page lets you manage your calendar.

To use the calendar, click the Calendar button.

Managing Your Calendar

Add an Event

To add a new event to your calendar, perform the following steps:

1. Click the date of the event on the calendar. You can navigate through different months using the buttons at the top.
2. Click the **New Item** button. A popup window will appear.
3. Give the event a name.

4. Using the checkboxes, select what type of event you are creating. If it is a birthday or anniversary, the computer will remember these events each year, and you can skip ahead to step **9**. If it is an appointment or other type of event, continue to step **5**.
5. Click in the box to the right of the word **Location,** then type in a location for the event.
6. Enter a time for the event to start.
7. Select the duration of the event to indicate how long the event will last.
8. Click the **Reminder** droplist to set the reminder for the alarm. The **Reminder** is the amount of time before the event that you want the alarm to go off. Select **None** to set no alarm.
9. If it is a recurring event, click the **Frequency** droplist to select how often you would like the event to occur.

View Event Details

To view or change the details for an existing event on your calendar, follow these instructions:

1. Click the day of the event you would like to view. The event will appear in the **Daily Reminders** section.
2. Click the event in the **Daily Reminders** section. A pop-up window will appear displaying the settings and notes for that event.
3. At this point you may edit the information and click **Save** when you are done, or click **Cancel** to exit with no saved changes.

Edit an Event

To edit the details for an existing event on your calendar, follow these instructions:

1. Click the day of the event which needs to be edited. The event will appear in the **Daily Reminders** section.
2. Click the event in the **Daily Reminders** section. A pop-up window will appear with the settings for that event.
3. Make the appropriate changes and click **Save**.

Remove an Event

To remove an existing event on your calendar, follow these instructions:

1. Click the day of the event in the calendar. The event will appear in the **Daily Reminders** section.
2. Click the event in the **Daily Reminders** section. A pop-up window will appear with the settings for that event.
3. Click the **Delete** button. You will be asked to confirm the action.

Dismiss/Snooze a Reminder

When you set a reminder for an event and the reminder comes due, a window will open on your screen. You may either dismiss or snooze the reminder.

To dismiss a reminder, simply click the **Dismiss** button.

To snooze the reminder, click the **Snooze** button - this is like hitting the snooze button on an alarm clock. The reminder window will disappear and reappear again in about 5 minutes.

Contacts

Your contacts are stored in an Address Book that is similar to one you might keep at home. You can manage your contacts easily with the Address Book by storing addresses, phone numbers and other important information. You can also use your address book to easily email your contacts.

To use your Address Book and manage contacts, click the Contacts Button.
When you click the Contacts button, your Address Book is displayed. You will notice it looks very much like a real address book, complete with alphabetic tabs to allow you to organize and navigate through your list of contacts.

Alphabetic Tabs

Your contacts are stored in alphabetical order by last name. Use the alphabetic tabs to navigate through your contacts. For example, if the contact's last name is **"Smith"**, click the Q-S tab.

If you don't have a lot of contacts, you may see them all listed when you click alphabetic tabs that do not contain the first letter of a contact's last name. This is okay. The Address Book is designed to allow you to see all your contacts in this situation.

Left and Right Pages

Your electronic Address Book is organized a little differently than a traditional address book. You'll notice it has a **left page** and a **right page**. The left page is used to display a list of your contacts and the right page is used to display your contact's information. Once you begin adding contacts, you will see them listed in the left page. To display a contact's information, click the contact's name and you will see their details displayed in the right page. On the left page, you may notice some icons under some of your contacts' names. Below is a list of icons and meanings.

- ✉ - This contact has an email address saved in your address book.
- f - This contact is one of your Facebook friends.
- 🗨 - This contact is one of your Skype contacts.

Contacts, Requests & Removed

The Address Book also displays three buttons at the top of the left page: Contacts, Requests and Removed. Clicking these buttons will change the function of the Address Book. The default function is Contacts to allow you to add, view, edit and remove contacts.

If you have removed (blocked) a Facebook or Skype contact, click the Removed button to view these contacts and to restore them, if you wish. See the section below for restoring blocked Facebook/Skype contacts.

The Requests button allows you to view contact requests from Facebook and Skype and to accept or ignore these requests. See the section below for accepting contact requests.

Managing Contacts

Add a Contact
1. Click **Add**
2. On the right page, enter the information for your new contact
3. Click **Save Contact** when you are done

View a Contact
1. Use the alphabetic tabs to navigate to the contact
2. Click the name of the contact
3. On the right page, you will see the contact's information

Below the contact's information is the **Video Chat** button. If this person is a Skype contact, clicking this button will allow you to see this contact's Skype name.

Edit a Contact
1. Use the alphabetic tabs to navigate to the contact
2. Click the contact's name to display their information on the right page
3. Make changes or additions to that contact's information. The information is automatically saved once you enter it

Remove a Contact

You can permanently remove a contact if it is not a Facebook or Skype contact. Once removed, the contact cannot be restored, so use with caution. See the sections below for handling Facebook and Skype contacts. To remove a contact, follow these instructions:

1. Use the alphabetic tabs to navigate to the contact
2. Click the contact's name to display their information on the right page
3. Click the **Remove** button. You will be asked to confirm the action

Add/Change a Photo
1. Use the alphabetic tabs to navigate to the contact
2. Click the contact's name to display their information on the right page
3. Click the **Change Photo** button

4. A window will appear to allow you to browse through your local albums or through that contact's Facebook albums. Click the photo you would like to use and select the **OK** button.

Email or Call a Contact

If you have entered an email address for a contact, you may click **Email** on the right page to address an email to them!

Similarly, if you are a Skype contact with a contact, you may click **Video Call** to start a **Video Chat** call with them! Clicking the **Audio Call** button will start a voice call to the person. Remember, the person you want to call must be online and logged into Skype to answer.

Duplicate Contacts

If there are two contacts in your address book that have the same name, using the **Duplicates?** button, located at the bottom right corner of the **left** page, will allow you to merge the two contact entries. If there is conflicting information in the two entries (example: Contact 1 has the Home phone number as (555) 565-5459 and Contact 2 has the Home phone number as (557) 544-5085), you will be given a popup to let you choose what information you would like to keep.

Importing Email Contacts

Importing Contacts from Gmail

If you have contacts saved on your Gmail contacts you can import them to your address book by following these instructions:

1. Click Web.
2. Log in to Gmail via webmail.
3. Click Contacts tab on left side of the webpage.
4. Click More.
5. Click Export...
6. Select the vCard format
7. Click Export.

Download will happen within a few seconds and the contacts will be imported automatically.

Importing Contacts from Yahoo!

If you have contacts saved on your Yahoo! contacts you can import them to your address book by following these instructions:

1. Click Web.
2. Login to Yahoo! webmail.
3. Click Contacts tab on the webpage.

4. Click Actions button on the top menu bar.
5. Select Export All...
6. Select vCard Single File option.
7. Enter the Captcha code correctly.

Download will happen in roughly 5 seconds and the contacts will be imported automatically.

Managing Facebook/Skype Contacts

Facebook and Skype contacts are added through contact requests. You may send or receive contact requests. When you accept a contact request that is sent to you, the contact will automatically be added to your **Address Book**.

View Contact Requests

The **Requests** button allows you to view your Facebook and Skype contact requests. When you are viewing your **Address Book**, simply click the **Requests** button at the top of the left page. You will see a list of contact requests displayed, along with the type of request: Facebook or Skype.

Alternately... when you receive a contact request, a notice will appear in the **Notices** section of the **Home** screen. Clicking this notice will take you to the list of your requests - similar to clicking the **Requests** button.

Accept a Contact Request

The **Requests** button allows you to view and accept your Facebook and Skype contact requests. To accept a contact request, follow these instructions:

1. Click the **Requests** button at the top of the left page of the **Address Book**. You will see a list of contact requests displayed, along with the type of request: Facebook or Skype.
2. Click the name of the contact whose request you want to accept.
3. You will be presented with a series of prompts to accept the request and add the contact. Follow the prompts to accept the request and add the person as a new or existing contact.

Block a Facebook/Skype Contact

You cannot permanently remove Facebook or Skype contacts. Both Facebook and Skype impose this restriction. Instead, the contact will be "blocked" and moved to the **Removed** list. To block a Facebook or Skype contact, follow these instructions:

1. Use the alphabetic tabs to navigate to the contact
2. Click the contact's name to display their information on the right page
3. Click the **Remove** button. You will be asked to confirm the action

View Blocked Facebook/Skype Contacts

The **Removed** button allows you to view any Facebook or Skype contacts that you may have blocked. To view blocked contacts, follow these instructions:

1. Click the **Removed** button at the top of the **Address Book**
2. You will see a list of all blocked Facebook and/or Skype contacts

Restore Blocked Facebook/Skype Contacts

The Removed button allows you to view and restore Facebook or Skype contacts that you have removed. To restore a contact, follow these instructions:

1. Click the **Removed** button at the top of the **Address Book**
2. Click the name of the contact you wish to restore
3. Click **Restore**
4. Click **Yes** when asked if you want to activate the contact

Weather

This application allows you to view weather conditions for a specific zip code or city, as well as providing you with a 5 day forecast and a Doppler map.

If this is your first time using weather, enter your zip code in the box where it says Please enter your zip code here for your profile and then click the Save to Profile button. Once you have saved your zip code into your profile, whenever you click the Weather button, the weather for your zip code will automatically be displayed.

To change the zip code in your profile, follow these instructions:

1. Click the **Settings** button, located in the top right corner of the screen
2. Click the **General Settings** button, located in the top right corner of the screen
3. Click the **My Profile** button, located at the top of the column of buttons on the right
4. Change the zip code in the field labeled Zip
5. Click **Save Changes**
6. Click Close, which is the red button near the top right corner of the screen

To check weather for other cities, enter the zip code or name of the city in the white box to the left of the green **GO** button and then click **GO**. If there is more than one city with that name then you will be given a list of cities, states/provinces, and countries from which to choose.

Click this button: to return to the weather for the zip code set in your profile.

Current Conditions

This section displays general information about current weather conditions for the selected zip code, including temperature in degrees Fahrenheit or Celsius (see below for details), chance of precipitation, and forecasts for day and evening. Other useful weather information given includes:

- Humidity

- Barometer
- Wind
- RealFeel
- Visibility

Weather Map

The live Doppler radar map displays an animated view of the weather patterns for the selected zip code. If the location searched is outside the United States, the map will show a satellite view instead.

5 Day Forecast

At the bottom of your screen, you will see a 5-day forecast for the selected zip code. Click any day to display a more detailed forecast for that day in the **Current Conditions** section.

Changing Temperature Output

The temperatures are displayed in degrees Fahrenheit by default but you can change it to degrees Celsius by following these instructions:

1. If you are not already in the Weather application, click the **Weather** button; otherwise, skip to step 2.
2. Click the **Settings** button in the upper right-hand corner of the screen.
3. Select the temperature output that you would like your weather to be in (i.e. Fahrenheit or Celsius). A check mark will appear in the box next to the selected output.
4. After making your selection, click **Close**, which is located in the upper right-hand corner of the screen.

News

News allows you to view a list of updated headlines from various news sources available on the Internet. You must have a working internet connection to use the News application.

To read the news, click the News button.

Welcome to your electronic newspaper! When you click the **News** button, you will see a list of news headlines and a list of news category buttons along the right side of the headlines. Simply click a news headline to read the article. Click a category button to view headlines in that category - similar to browsing through different sections of the newspaper.

News Source

Your electronic newspaper allows you to change the source of the news. This is similar to choosing a different newspaper to read. The current news source is displayed at the top right corner of the list of headlines. Examples of news sources are Yahoo, CNN and ESPN. See the section below for changing the news source.

Change News Source/Category

To change the news source, follow these instructions:
1. Click **Change News Source**
2. Click the name of any news source.
3. Click **OK**.

You will see the headlines, news source and category buttons update to reflect your selection.

Change News Category

The category buttons are listed along the right side of the news headlines page. Click any category button to list the headlines for a particular category. For instance, if you clicked **Politics**, you will see the latest politics-related headlines from your selected news source.

Reading Articles

When you click a news headline to read the full story, the article will appear with function buttons across the top. When reading an article, you may use these buttons to add the article to your favorites, print it out, navigate or zoom in/out. When you are finished reading and want to view the headlines again, click the Back to News button to go back to the last page of headlines that you viewed.

Back to News

Click Back to News to return to the news headlines page.

 Back

Click Back to view the previous web page.

 Forward

Click Next to view the next web page.

 Add to Favorites

Click the **Add to Favorites** button to bookmark the site you are currently viewing. A pop-up window will appear so that you can edit the information for the bookmark. You can use the default name that appears in the **Name** field, or give your bookmark a unique name. You can also save the bookmark into an existing category using the **category** drop down menu, or create a new one in the "Or enter new" field.

Click **Ok** to add the bookmark, or **Cancel** to cancel adding the bookmark.

 Print

If you have a printer connected to your computer, click this button to print the current page.

 Zoom In/Out

Clicking these buttons will increase or decrease the size of the article, making it easier to read.

Web

Use the Web application to view web sites with the built in web browser.

To use the internet, click the Web button.

The Web application allows you to visit any web site on the Internet. You can also bookmark any site so that you can easily return to it at a later time. When you first enter the Web application, you will see the Quick Links page (see below). You can either click one of these sites to visit, or type in any other address in the address bar (see below.)

Web Toolbar Buttons

Quick Links

Click this button to view the Quick Links page. This page displays some of the most useful and popular websites, grouped by category. Within each category are icons for the web sites that make up that category. You may need to move the slider down in order to see all of the categories.

To view one of the web sites, click the icon for that web site. For example, click to go to that website.

If you change your Home Page, clicking this button will take you to that page in place of the Quick Links page. To change your Home Page, follow these instructions:

1. Click *Web*.
2. Click *Settings*, located next to the *Help* button in the upper right-hand corner of your screen. This will bring up the *Browser Settings* page
3. Click the *Home Page:* text field.
4. Type the URL of the website you want to set as your new Home Page.

TECH TIP: *If the website you want to set as your new Home Page is long or difficult to remember, then navigate to that page and use keyboard controls (instructions listed below) to copy and paste the URL into this field.*

5. When you have either typed or pasted the URL into the text field, click the *Save*.
6. If you ever wish to change your Home Page back to the Quick Links page, click the *Use Quick Links* button on the *Browser Settings* page then click *Save*.

NOTE: *Please be aware that if the website you set as your Home Page falls under a category that is blocked by the Web Filter then clicking this button will not take you to that page.*

Favorites

The Favorites button will take you to your list of bookmarked sites. These can also be organized into categories, which can be renamed at any time by clicking **Edit**, typing a new name and clicking **Done**. To navigate to a bookmarked website, click the **Favorites** button then click the name of the website that you've bookmarked. You can bookmark any website by clicking the **Add to Favorites** button (see below).

 Back

Click **Back** to view the previous web page.

 Forward

Click **Forward** after using the Back button to return to the next web page.

 Add to Favorites

Click the **Add to Favorites** button to bookmark the site you are currently viewing. A pop-up window will appear so that you can edit the information for the bookmark. You can use the default name that appears in the **Name** field, or give your bookmark a unique name. You can also save the bookmark into an existing category using the **category** drop down menu, or create a new one in the "Or enter new" field.

Click **Ok** to add the bookmark, or **Cancel** to cancel adding the bookmark.

Address Bar

The **Address Bar** is used to enter the URL, or address, of a website. To navigate to a specific web site, type the web site name, for example "www.yahoo.com" or "www.google.com", into the **Address Bar** and then click the **GO** button.

Additionally, the **Address Bar** can be used to search the Internet. Simply type in a company name or name of a person, place or thing into the **Address Bar**, then click **GO** to generate a list of search results for that word. In the search results list, click the blue underlined text to view a website that matches your search. When searching, you may enter a single word or combination of words into the **Address Bar**.

 Print

If you have a printer connected to your computer, click this button to print the current page.

 Zoom In

To magnify or enlarge the words and pictures on a web site, click the **Zoom In** button.

 Zoom Out

To reduce the words and pictures on a web site, fitting more on the page, click the **Zoom Out** button.

Keyboard Controls

Functions like **Cut**, **Copy**, and **Paste** can be utilized by using a combination of keystrokes. To Cut or Copy, simply highlight the text you wish to duplicate. Then:

- Simultaneously press **ctrl**, located in the bottom left corner of your keyboard, and "C", if you want to **Copy** the text.

- Simultaneously press ctrl and "X", if you want to **Cut** the text.

To **Paste** text that you have copied or cut, simply click where you would like to place the text, then simultaneously press ctrl and "V".

NOTE: Keyboard Controls can only be utilized by using a real keyboard; the on-screen keyboard will not work.

TECH TIP: Using copy on a webpage is recommended over the use of the cut function because the cut function only works for text you typed yourself.

Saving Pictures from the Web

To save pictures from the web, click the picture with your right mouse button. This will bring up a dialog box that says, "Do you want to save this image into an album?" Click the Ok button. You will then be given the option to select which album you wish to save the image in. When you have chosen the album you wish to put the image in, click Save, or if you wish to create a new album for it, click the New Album button, type the name of the album you wish to create, and click Ok. If at any time you change your mind about a decision, click Cancel

Games

For game functionality and rules:
- **Click the Games button**
- **Click the icon for the game that you would like instruction**
- **Click the Help button in the upper right corner of the screen**

More

This area lists additional applications available on your computer.

To view more applications available on your computer, click the More button.

Backup/Restore

Backup/Restore is a feature that allows you to easily backup your computer's information on an external hard disc - or on our server computers - for safekeeping. You may also easily restore your backed up information with this feature.

To use the Backup / Restore application:
- **Click the More button**
- **Click the Backup/Restore icon**

There are two ways to perform backups: locally or via the network. Network backup/restore is a paid service, where your files are stored on our server computers. It's easier to use, because backups will be done automatically - you don't need an external hard disc and only need to leave your computer on - and the backup will be run on a regularly scheduled basis. Local backups are done using your own external hard disc. You will need to manually perform the backups, but we'll help you set up reminders if you want!

Local Backup/Restore

Local Backups

There are three simple steps to performing a local backup:

1. Attach an external hard disc.
2. Run the backup.
3. Disconnect the hard disc.

These steps are described in the sections below.

Attach the Hard Disc

Simply plug in an external hard disc into one of the USB ports located on the back and/or side of your computer. The computer will automatically recognize that you have connected the hard disc, and will start to scan the hard disc to see how much space is available for backup use. Once the amount of space available has been determined, if there's enough for your backup, the Backup Now button will become enabled, and you can move to the next step.

Backup Data

Simply click the Backup Now button and your backup will begin. First, the computer will determine what files need to be backed up. You'll see a progress bar while this is happening. Next, the files will be saved to the attached hard disc. You will see another progress bar while the files are being backed up. When the progress bar disappears, your backup is finished!

Disconnect the Hard Disc

Once the progress bar has disappeared, unplug your hard disc, and put it in a safe place. Be sure you don't remove the hard disc until the progress bar has gone away, though.

Setting Backup Reminders

You can have your computer remind you to do backups on a regular basis. You can schedule these reminders to be once a week or once a month. On the **Backup/Restore** settings screen, simply click the check box next to the frequency of the reminder you want. When a reminder is set, it will appear in the **Notices** section of your **Home** screen. If you want to change the date that these reminders appear in your **Notices**, click **Calendar**, click the day the reminder currently occurs, then click the reminder to open it for editing.

Restoring Data

If you ever need to restore backed up files onto your computer, follow these instructions:

1. Click **Backup/Restore**.
2. Attach your external backup disc.
3. Click **Restore Now** and your files will be copied back to your computer.

Network Backup/Restore

This is a paid service. You will need to purchase a backup subscription to use it. It is very convenient to use, and your data is stored for you on our servers.

Purchasing a Network Backup/Restore Subscription

To subscribe to our network backup service, simply click the Purchase Subscription button. This will take you to a popup page that allows you to securely purchase a backup subscription.

Network Backup

Once you have subscribed to our network backup service, your computer will automatically backup files to our servers - without you having to do anything! If you need to backup at a particular time, you can just click **Network Backup Now**, and your computer will start the backup process.

NOTE: You may only click the Network Backup Now button once in a 24 hour period.

Network Restore

If you need to restore your data, all you need to do is click the Restore from Network button, and your files will be copied from our server to your computer. Once the restore has completed, you will be asked to restart your computer.

CD Player

This application allows you to listen to CDs that you have inserted into the computer's disk drive. You can have your CD play in the background while you use the computer's other functions.

To use the CD application:
- **Click the More button**
- **Click the CD Player icon**

Album Art

If you are connected to the internet then the album art for your CD will appear in the box in the top left corner. If you are not connected to the internet then a default picture and the words "no album art found" will appear in the box in the top left corner.

Track List

This is a list of all audio tracks on your CD and the length of each track. If you are connected to the internet then the list will show the track titles; however if you do not have an internet connection then the title will appear as the track number. The track list not only shows you what tracks are on your CD but also lets you select a specific track to play. To choose a track you want to play, click the title of the track. The icon to the left of the track title shows its current play status.

▶ Indicates that the current track is not playing

♫ Indicates that the current track is playing

Now Playing

Located just beneath the **Track List** is the Now Playing info panel. This shows you what track is currently playing, how long the track is, and how far into the track you are. If Shuffle and/or Repeat are activated then it will be displayed in this panel to the right of current track title.

Artist: / Album:

Located beneath the **Album Art** are the Artist and Album information. If you are connected to the internet, these will tell you the name of the artist and album that you are currently playing.

To insert a CD, press the small button on the CD tray, or, if you are in the **CD Player** application, click **Eject CD**. When the tray pops open, place your CD in the tray, pressing firmly around the center until you hear or feel it snap on. Then gently press the tray in toward the computer to close. You will hear a click when the tray is closed. It should close easily and require only gentle pressure. Never force a disc into the tray.

NOTE: Before pressing the tray in, ensure the disc is mounted firmly on the tray. If the disc is loose or falling off the tray, then it is not mounted properly and you run the risk of damaging the tray and possibly the drive.

Playing a CD

Playing a CD is easy! Simply insert a CD into the computer and you will be prompted to play the CD. If you are in the CD Player application, just click the play button. CD function buttons are described below.

CD Player Function Buttons

Located beneath the Now Playing info panel are several buttons. These buttons are used to control the playing of the CD.

 Play — The play button serves two purposes. If you have a CD in your disk drive and the CD player is not currently running, pressing Play will start the application. If a track is paused, clicking Play will resume play.

 Pause — If a track is currently playing, the Play button will change to a Pause button. Clicking Pause will pause the track at whatever point in the track you are, clicking play will continue the track from that point.

Stop — The stop button turns off the CD Player.

 Previous Track / Replay — This button allows you to go to the track that is listed directly before the current track on the Track List; however if the current track is the first track, clicking this button will bring you to the last track on the Track List. If you are more than 5 seconds into the current track, then clicking this button will restart the current track.

 Next Track — This button allows you to go to the track that is listed directly after the current track on the Track List; however if the current track is the last track, then clicking this button will bring you to the first on the Track List

Shuffle — Clicking Shuffle activates Shuffle mode. When Shuffle mode is activated, the tracks will play in a random order; however the Previous Track button will play the track played before the current track.

Repeat — Repeat allows you to choose what happens when a track finishes playing.
- Clicking Repeat once will set it so that track restarts when it finishes playing. The display will read, "Repeat One".
- Clicking Repeat twice will set it so that it plays the next track on the list, but after the last track finishes playing, it will replay all of the tracks. The display will read, "Repeat All".
- Clicking **Repeat** three times will turn off the Repeat feature. The display will be blank.
- If **Repeat** is not on, then the CD Player will turn off when the last

	track finishes playing.
Eject	Clicking Eject will open the disk drive.
Back	Located in the top right corner, the Back button will take you back to the More main page; however if you do not click Stop before clicking Back the CD Player will continue to play.

Calculator

Use the calculator to perform basic math calculations. When you click the equals button (=), a running tab will be displayed to the right of the calculator. Below is a list of the calculator's functions.

Calculator Functions

Bksp	Delete one number at a time.
%	Determines a percentage. For example, 8% is .08 and is displayed as "8%".
1/x	Divides one by the number entered. For example, 5 then 1/x = 0.2
+/-	Change the number from positive to negative.
.	Adds a decimal point.
C	Clear - Clears the current line or entry.
AC	All Clear - Clears everything. All the past functions as well as the current line.
/	Divides two numbers. For example, 8 / 4 = 2
X	Multiplies two numbers. For example, 3 x 3 = 9
-	Subtracts two numbers. For example, 4 - 2 = 2
+	Adds two numbers. For example, 3 + 4 = 7
=	Determines the result of the current operation.

Alternate Input Method

Besides using the buttons on the screen, you can also use your keyboard to enter numbers and functions.

Conversion

This page allows you to convert measurements, weights, and distances between different units.

Converting Between Units

To convert between different units, perform the following steps:

1. Enter the measurement, weight, or distance that you would like to convert from.
2. Use the drop down menu ▼ to select the units you are converting from.
3. Use the drop down menu ▼ to select the units you would like to convert to.
4. Click the Go button.

NOTE: The conversion will be measured out to two decimal places.

 DVD Player

This is your computer's DVD player. You can watch videos that you insert into the computer's DVD tray.

To use the DVD Player:
- Click the More button
- Click the DVD Player icon

Inserting a DVD

To insert a DVD, press the small button on the DVD tray, or, if you are in the DVD Player application, click "Please insert a DVD". When the tray pops open, place your DVD in the tray, pressing firmly around the center until you hear or feel it snap on. Then gently press the tray in toward the computer to close. You will hear a click when the tray is closed. It should close easily and require only gentle pressure. Never force a disc into the tray.

NOTE: Before pressing the tray in, ensure the disc is mounted firmly on the tray. If the disc is loose or falling off the tray, then it is not mounted properly and you run the risk of damaging the tray and possibly the drive.

Watching a DVD

Watching a DVD is easy! Simply insert a DVD into the computer and you will be prompted to play the movie. If you are in the DVD Player application, just click Play Movie.

Ejecting a DVD

To eject a DVD that is in the DVD tray, click **Open DVD Tray**.

DVD Player Toolbar

Once you have inserted a DVD and clicked Play Movie, the movie will begin to play and you will see the DVD toolbar appear at the bottom of the screen. Use this toolbar to access DVD functions and to control the playback of the DVD. The following functions are available from your DVD toolbar:

Menu

If the DVD has menu options, click the **Menu** button to display a list of the available options for the video. Menu options may include chapter and scene selection, subtitles and bonus features.

▷	**Play**	Click to start or continue playing the DVD. It will then change to the Pause button.
❚❚	**Pause**	Click to pause the DVD at the current position. It will then change to the Play Button.
■	**Stop**	Click the **Stop** button to stop the video and exit. To play, select **Play Video**.
▷▷	**Fast Forward**	Click the **Fast Forward** button to fast forward the video. The video will continue to fast forward until you click the Play button.
◁◁	**Rewind**	Click the **Rewind** button to rewind the video. The video will continue to rewind until you click the Play button.
▷▷❘	**Next Chapter**	Click the **Next Chapter** button to skip ahead to the next chapter.
❘◁◁	**Previous Chapter**	Click the **Previous Chapter** button to skip back to the previous chapter.
⬤	**Volume**	Drag the volume slider left or right to lower or raise the volume.

Subtitles

If the video has subtitles, select the **Subtitles** button to toggle the subtitles on or off.

 # File Manager

The File Manager allows you to manage the files and folders on your computer. You may move files, delete files and create new folders.

To use the File Manager:
- **Click the More button**
- **Click the File Manager icon**

Files & Folders

There are many types of files: documents, images, PDFs, etc. For example, the Write application is used to create documents and you may get image attachments in email. The File Manager is used to move, copy, and delete files.

Your computer uses folders as a way to organize your files. For example, you may create a "Taxes" folder to store documents that are related to your taxes. The File Manager is used to move, delete or create new folders.

Source & Destination panels

The File Manager has two panels: **From** and **To**. The files and folders on your computer are displayed in these panels.

The **From** panel is used to select files/folders to be moved, copied, or deleted. The **To** panel is where you will select a destination folder for moved or copied files.

Using the File Manager

Create a Folder

Click the **New Folder** button to create a new folder in the **To** panel. Enter a name and click **OK**.

Select a File/Folder

To select a file or folder, simply click the check box: ✓ to the left of file's or folder's name. If you wish to select all of the files in the current folder, click the topmost checkbox.

Rename a File/Folder

To rename a file or folder, simply select a file or folder, then click Rename. A dialog box will appear to allow you to type a new name for your file or folder. If you are satisfied with the new name clicking Ok will save the change; however if you wish to keep the name the same, clicking Cancel will restore the original name.

Delete a File/Folder

In the **From** panel, select the file(s) or folder(s) you want to delete, and then click the **Delete** button. You will be asked to confirm the delete.

NOTE: When a folder is deleted, all the contents of that folder will be deleted. Please use delete with caution.

Move a File/Folder

When you want to move a file or folder, follow these instructions:
1. Find the file/folder you want to move in the **From** panel and select it.
2. Find the destination folder in the **To** panel and click it.

3. Click **Move**.

Copy a File/Folder

When you want to move a file or folder, follow the instructions:

1. Find the file/folder you want to copy in the **From** panel and select it.
2. Find the destination folder in the **To** panel and click it.
3. Click **Copy**

Open a Folder

To open a folder, click the folder name.

Open a File

To open a file, click the file name then click **Open**, located to the right of the active folder's name. The file will then open in the appropriate application.

If the file you are opening is an audio or video file, then the media player will appear in a popup, so that you will be able to listen to or view that file.

Back button

If you have opened a folder and want to return to the previous folder, click the ◀ button, located to the left of the current folder name.

Major Folders

NOTE: ***These folders cannot be deleted.***

Documents

This folder is the default location for saving text-based files. These include, but are not limited to: Write/Word documents, slideshows, and PDFs

Photos

This folder is the default location for saving picture files. This folder also contains all your locally saved photo albums. Clicking on an album's folder will allow you to see thumbnails of the pictures in that album's folder. You can also select pictures in order to **Copy** or **Move** them to a different folder. If you **Rename** an album's folder, it will also rename the corresponding album, with the exception of the Favorites album.

USB

This folder will only appear if you have an external hard drive or USB flash drive, also referred to as a thumb drive or memory stick, or a camera memory card, plugged into your computer. Clicking on this folder will show you all the files that are saved on the USB device. You will be able to **Copy** and **Move** files from the device to your computer and vice versa.

Data Disc

This folder will only appear if you have a disc, with the exception of a music CD or a video DVD, in the disk drive. Clicking on this folder will show you all the files that are saved on the Disc, and you will be able to **Copy** files to your computer. When this folder is selected but not open an **Eject** button will appear next to the **Open** button. Clicking this will open the disc tray so that you may remove the disc from your computer.

 # Kindle Reader

The **Kindle Reader** application will allow you to read eBooks (electronic books) and listen to audio books on your computer that you purchase from Amazon.com! This will require you to have - or create - an Amazon.com account. Amazon.com is the largest bookseller on the internet. Opening an account with Amazon.com is free, but you will need to purchase the eBooks to read them on your computer. If you have a Kindle device, any books you purchase on Amazon.com can be read on both your Kindle and your computer.

Getting Started

To use the Kindle Reader, you will need an email address to create an.com account. If you do not have an email address, please create one and then return.

When you first open the Kindle Reader application, you will be presented with the "Sign In" screen.

Create an Account

If you do not have an account, you may create one now.

1. Enter your email address in the email of the Sign In screen
2. Click the circle next to "I am a new customer"
3. Click the button labeled, "Sign In using our secure server"
4. Enter your name, your email address again, and a password (twice)
5. Click "Create account"

You will be able to access the Kindle Reader now.

Sign In

If you have an Amazon.com account, you can sign in now. Enter your email address and password into the fields of the Sign In screen, and then click the button labeled, "Sign In using our secure server".

You may need to click the "Get Started Now" button.

You will be able to access the Kindle Reader now.

Kindle Library

When you sign into your Amazon.com account, you will be presented with your library. If you have purchased books or have borrowed books from the Library (requires a Library card and PIN from your preferred branch), you will see them here. Simply click a book to begin reading it!

Library Toolbar

The library toolbar contains icons for tools you can click to manage your library of books.

Sync

Click this button to synchronize the Kindle Reader with your Kindle device.

Settings

Click this button to get Help or Sign Out.

Search

Click this button to search through your library for a particular book. You may search by author or book title.

Kindle Store

Click the "Kindle Store" button to go to the Amazon.com website. This is where you may purchase new eBooks to read on your computer. Click the "Reader" button at the top of the screen to get back to your reader at any time.

Local Library

Some local libraries will allow you to borrow e-books on-line for a set period of time. You can then read or listen to these e-books on your computer or download them to your Kindle device. To find out how to borrow books from your library follow these instructions:

1. Call or visit your local library to find out if they offer e-books.
2. Confirm that you have a library account (card and PIN number) with that library.

3. Go to your local library website and locate the eBooks section (some libraries may call this Digital Downloads, Download Books, Digital Content or OverDrive). If you are having difficulty finding this section, it is recommended that you ask a librarian for help or call your library and ask for instructions.
4. Search for and check out your Kindle book selections. When prompted, log in with your library card ID (and PIN, if required). If you need to request a hold on a title, use your personal e-mail address to make the hold.
5. Once you've checked out your title, choose **Get for Kindle**. You'll be redirected to Amazon.com's Public Library Loan page for that title. (You may be required to log in to your Amazon.com account -- or create a new account -- if you're not already logged in). Choose your device from the **Deliver to** menu, and choose **Get library book** to send the book to your reading app or device.

Reading Books

Overview

Once you are reading a book, simply click the arrows to the left or right of the text to turn the page backwards or forwards. The progress bar at the bottom of the screen shows you how far into the book you are.

Book Toolbar

The book toolbar contains icons for tools you can use while you are reading one of your books.

Library

Click this button to return to your library of books.

Show/Hide Toolbar

Click this button to show or hide the book toolbar.

Navigate

Click this button for navigation options. You will be able to navigate to the following locations in the book:

- Cover
- Table of Contents
- Beginning
- Location... (a specific page)
- Book Extras (additional information about the book and/or author)

Format / Text Size

Click this button to access formatting options for the reader. You will be able to change the following options:

1. Font Size (size of the letters)
2. Margins
3. Color Mode (black text on white background -OR- brown text on sepia background -OR- white text on black background)

Click "Apply Settings" to confirm your changes, or click "Cancel" to ignore changes.

Bookmark

 Click this button to add a bookmark. A bookmark will be added to the page:

Click any bookmark to remove it.

To see all your bookmarks, click the "Note" button in the toolbar (see below).

Note

 Click this button to highlight text or to manage and go to your notes and bookmarks.

To create a note, click a word, or drag to select words, and then click "Note". This will open a window for you to type in a note. Click "Save" to save the note. Click "Cancel" to back out of the operation.

To highlight text, click a word, or drag to select words, and then click "Highlight".

To go to a bookmark or note, click the Note button on the toolbar, then click a bookmark or note.

Media Player

The Media Player lets you play and enjoy audio and video files that you have saved on your computer. You can watch videos or listen to music, using this application, or have music playing in the background while you enjoy the other features your computer has to offer.

Making a Playlist

A playlist is a user-created list of media files, and lets you listen or watch these files without having to search through all of your files. The buttons below the **Pick the playlist** selection window can be used to create, rename, or delete playlist(s). The buttons are:

Add

Use this button to create a playlist. After clicking this button, a popup will appear asking you to "Enter the name of the new playlist". Type a name for your playlist, then click the green **OK** button. You can use the **Add** button to create as many playlists as you want.

Rename

Use this button to change the name of a playlist. Select the playlist you wish to rename from the **Pick the playlist** selection window; then click the **Rename** button. After clicking this button, a popup will appear asking you to "Enter the new name of the playlist". Type a name for your playlist, then click the green **OK** button.

Remove

Use this button to delete a playlist. Select the playlist you wish to rename from the **Pick the playlist** selection window; then click the **Remove** button.

Managing a Playlist

After creating a playlist, you can then fill it with your audio and video files so that you can play them. The buttons at the top of the playlist are:

Add Media

Use this button to add music and videos to a playlist. To do this, follow these instructions:

1. Click **More**.
2. Click **Media Player**.
3. Select a playlist from the **Pick a playlist** selection window.
4. Click the **Add Media** button.
5. After clicking Add Media, an **Open File** popup will appear. Select the file(s) you want by click the check box next to the file's name.
6. After you have chosen the file(s) you want to add to your playlist, click the green **Open** button.

Tech Tip: Only files in the Multimedia folder can be added to a playlist. If you have media files in saved in other folders that you would like in your playlist, go to the **File Manager** and move them to the Multimedia folder.

Remove Media

Use this button to remove music or videos from a playlist. Select the song or video you wish to remove from your playlist; then click the **Remove Media** button. This will remove the file from your playlist, but you can add it back at any time using the **Add Media** button.

Move Up / Move Down

Use these buttons to change the order in which your songs are played. **Move Up** moves the selected file towards the top of the list, and **Move Down** moves the selected file towards the bottom of the list.

Enjoying your Media

When you want to enjoy music or a video, select a playlist to play from or select the **All** playlist, which contains all of your media files. The buttons used to play your music and videos are:

Play

Clicking the **Play** button will start a song or video that has been selected from the current playlist or continue the song or video that is currently paused. If there is no song or video selected, the first item in the playlist will start.

 Pause

If there is already a song or video playing, the **Play** button will switch to a **Pause** button. Clicking the **Pause** button will pause the current song or video.

 Stop

This button ends the current song or video. If a song or video is stopped, pressing the play button will start it from the beginning.

 Previous / Replay

This button switches from the song or video that is currently playing to the one that comes directly before it in the playlist; if the current song or video is the first item in the playlist, clicking this button will bring you to the last song or video in the playlist. If you are more than 5 seconds into the current song or video, then clicking this button will restart the current song or video, instead of starting the previous song or video.

 Next

This button switches from the song or video that is currently playing to the one that comes directly after it in the playlist; however if the current track is the last song or video in the playlist, then clicking this button will bring you to the first item in the playlist.

Shuffle

Clicking Shuffle activates Shuffle mode. When Shuffle mode is activated, the songs and/or videos will play in a random order. The **Next** button will skip to a random song or video, however the **Previous** button will play the song or video played before the current track.

Repeat

Repeat allows you to choose what happens when a song or video finishes playing.

- Clicking **Repeat** once will set it so that the current song or video restarts when it finishes playing. The display will read, "Repeat One".

- Clicking **Repeat** twice will set it so that it plays the next song or video on the list, but after the last track finishes playing, it will replay all of the tracks. The display will read, "Repeat All".

- Clicking **Repeat** three times will turn off the Repeat feature. The display will be blank.

- If **Repeat** is not on, then the Media Player will turn off when the last song or video finishes playing.

Video Viewing Window

Located below the **Pick a playlist** selection window is the **Video Viewing Window**. This is where any video file you wish to view will play.

Eject CD

If there is a CD in your disc drive, clicking this button will open the disc drive.

Back

Located in the top right corner, the **Back** button will take you back to the **More** main page. If you do not click **Stop** before clicking **Back,** the Media Player will continue to play.

Rotate

When playing certain types of video files, a **Rotate** button will appear below the **Video Viewing Window**. Clicking this button lets you rotate the video 90 degrees to the left; however the rotation will not take effect until the next time you play the video.

Supported File Formats

Below is a list of common audio and video file formats that are known to be supported by your computer. Be aware that there may be other formats that will work with your computer but these formats are guaranteed.

- **Audio File Formats**

    - .mp3
    - .wma
    - .wav
    - .aac

- Video File Formats

    - .mpg
    - .wmv
    - .mov
    - .mp4
    - .avi
    - .flv

PDF Viewer

This application allows you to view PDF files.

To use the PDF Viewer:
- Click the More button
- Click the PDF Viewer icon

A PDF file is a type of document. PDF stands for "Portable Document Format". PDF files are commonly used on the Internet to display information. Examples of PDF files are IRS tax forms, bank statements, instruction manuals and articles.

PDF files can be viewed on the Internet or downloaded to your computer for later viewing. This application allows you to view PDF files on the Internet and also download them to your computer.

PDF Viewer Functions

	Open	Click **Open** to select the PDF file you would like to view. The **File Browser** will open, displaying the files/folders in your computer. If you have downloaded a PDF from an email sent to you, or from the Internet, you will find that PDF in your "Documents" folder. Select the PDF you would like to open, and then click **Open** in the **File Browser**.
	Close	When you are finished with viewing a PDF file, click **Close**, and the PDF file will close.
	Save As	If you want save a copy of the PDF file you are viewing, click **Save As**. The **File Browser** will open, displaying the files in your computer. You may select a new destination and name for the file. Click **Save** in the **File Browser** when you are done.
🔍+	**Zoom In**	Click this button to magnify the size of the display in the PDF file.
🔍−	**Zoom Out**	Click this button to reduce the size of the display in the PDF file.
↻	**Rotate Right**	Click this button to rotate the displayed PDF file to the right.
↺	**Rotate Left**	Click this button to rotate the displayed PDF file to the left.
🖨	**Print**	Click this button to print the current file
◀	**Previous Page**	Click this button to go to the previous page in the PDF file.
▶	**Next Page**	Click this button to go to the next page in the PDF file.

Photo Loader

The Photo Loader allows you to import photos from your media to your computer. You may create new Albums and import photos into them.

To use the Photo Loader application:
- Click the More button
- Click the Photo Loader icon

Files & Folders

There are many types of files: documents, images, PDFs, etc. The Photo loader will only show images and folders. There may be other documents on the media but they will be hidden so you can easily select photos and put them into the albums.

Source & Destination panels

The File Manager has two panels: **From** and **To**. The files and folders on your computer are displayed in these panels.

The **From** panel is used to select files/folders to be moved, copied, or deleted. It shows you all the removable media that you have attached to the computer. You can have memory sticks, data CDs or memory cards. The **To** panel is where you will select a destination folder for moved or copied files. It shows you all the local photo albums you have already created. You can create new ones or select existing ones in this panel.

Using the File Manager

Note: Some actions are not available depending on the media that is being imported. For instance you cannot create, rename or delete files or folders on CDs or locked media.

Create a Folder

Click the **New Folder** button to create a new folder in the **To** panel. Enter a name and click **OK**.

Select a File/Folder

To select a file or folder, simply click the check box: ✓ to the left of file's or folder's name. If you wish to select all of the files in the current folder, click the topmost checkbox.

Rename a File/Folder

To rename a file or folder, simply select a file or folder, then click **Rename**. A dialog box will appear to allow you to type a new name for your file or folder. If you are satisfied with the new name clicking **Ok** will save the change; however if you wish to keep the name the same, clicking **Cancel** will restore the original name.

Delete a File/Folder

In the ***From*** panel, select the file(s) or folder(s) you want to delete, and then click the ***Delete*** button. You will be asked to confirm the delete.

Note: When a folder is deleted, all the contents of that folder will be deleted. Please use delete with caution.

Move a File/Folder
1. When you want to move a file or folder, follow these instructions:
2. Find the file/folder you want to move in the ***From*** panel and select it.
3. Find the destination folder in the ***To*** panel and click it.
4. Click ***Move***.

Copy a File/Folder
1. When you want to move a file or folder, follow the instructions:
2. Find the file/folder you want to copy in the ***From*** panel and select it.
3. Find the destination folder in the ***To*** panel and click it.
4. Click Copy

Open a Folder

To open a folder, click the folder name.

Open a File

To open a file, click the file name then click ***Open***, located to the right of the active folder's name. The file will then open in the photo viewer.

If the file you are opening is an audio or video file, then the media player will appear in a popup, so that you will be able to listen to or view that file.

Back button

If you have opened a folder and want to return to the previous folder, click the ◀ button, located to the left of the current folder name.

Scanner

The Scanner application allows you to use your HP scanning printer to scan, copy, and save physical documents and photos as digital files.

To use the Photo Loader application:
- **Click the More button**
- **Click the Scanner icon**

Scanning Options

The ***Scanner*** application offers you two varieties of scanning described below.

Scan a Document

This option allows you to scan a document and save it as PDF file. To do so follow these instructions:

1. Click ***More***.
2. Click ***Scanner***.
3. Click the ***Scan a Document*** button. Your screen will change to the scanner setup page.
4. Place the document you wish to scan face down on your scanner, while making sure that the document is against the front and right corners of the glass.
5. Click the ***Scan*** button on your screen, which will start the scanning process.
6. When your scan is complete, the completed scan page will appear with the result of the scan. You can save this scan as a PDF file by clicking the ***Save Document*** button or discard the document by clicking ***Cancel***.
7. After clicking the Save This Scan button, a **Save File** popup will appear. Click the white box next to the word **Name**; then type a name for your file.
8. You can then choose a folder to place your file in or leave it in the documents folder, which is selected by default.
9. When you have selected a folder, click the green ***Save*** button. However, if you change your mind about wanting to save this file, click the red ***Cancel*** button.

Scan a Photo

This option allows you to scan a photo, allowing you more control over the end result, and then add it to one of your albums. To do so follow these options:

1. Click More.
2. Click Scanner.
3. Click the Scan a Photo button. Your screen will change to the scanner setup page.
4. Place the photo you wish to scan face down on your scanner, while making sure that the photo is against the front and right corners of the glass.
5. Click the Preview Scan on your screen, which will start the scanning process.
6. When the scanning process finishes, you will be given a Scan Preview which lets you adjust several aspects:
    - **Rotate** lets you rotate the photo 90 degrees to the **Right** or **Left**.
    - **Crop** allows you to choose the exact area of the photo you are scanning, eliminating empty borders. the several cropping options that are available to you are:
        - None, which means no cropping will be done.
        - 3.5 x 5

74

- 4 x 6
- 5 x 7
- 8 x 10
- Free, this allows you to arbitrarily adjust the size of the cropping area using the gray squares, located at the corners and edges of the area.

(Tech Tip: You can move the cropping area by clicking inside it and dragging it to the area of your choice.)

  o **Portrait** and **Landscape** are used to adjust the fixed crop sizes. For example, if you select 3.5 x 5 with portrait selected, the crop area will be 3.5 inches wide and 5 inches tall. If you select 3.5 x 5 with landscape selected, the crop area will be 5 inches wide and 3.5 inches tall.

7. When you have finished fine-tuning your scan, click Final Scan, which will rescan your photo with your adjustments.
8. When the scan is complete, click the Save Photo button. If you do not wish to save your scan, click the Cancel button.
9. After clicking the Save button, your photo albums will appear in a popup. Choose an album to place the photo in, then click Save.
10. After choosing an album, you should name your photo. A popup will appear asking you to "Enter a name for this photo:", click on the white box and type a name for your photo.
11. When you have finished typing a name for your photo, click the OK button.

Slideshow Viewer

This application allows you to view slideshow files (.ppt, .pptx, and .odp) that you have saved on your computer or that have been emailed to you as an attachment.

To use the Slideshow Viewer application:
- Click the More button
- Click the Slideshow Viewer icon

Slideshow Navigation Buttons

	Open	This button lets you view a previously saved slideshow.
◀	Previous	This button allows you to go to the previous slide in the slideshow
▶	Next	This button allows you to go to the next slide in the slideshow.
	Back	Located in the top right corner, the **Back** button will return you to the **More** main page.

Spreadsheets

This application allows you to view, edit, and create spreadsheet files. These files are saved in the ".xls" format and are compatible with Microsoft Excel. When you first start up the application, a new file with three blank sheets will be opened.

The following instructions assume that you have:
- Click the More button
- Click the Spreadsheets icon

Terms to know

Here is a list of terms and techniques used in this guide that are vital to know:

- Cell - Sheets are divided into columns (represented by letters) and rows (represented by numbers). Cells are the space formed by the overlapping of columns and rows, and are referred to by the column and row. For example a cell that is in the 4th column and 6th row is Cell D6. Cells can contain text, numbers, or functions.
- Highlight - To highlight cells, click and hold the left mouse button on a cell then move the cursor until all the cells you want to highlight are purple.
- Drag - You can move cells by dragging them to a new location. To do this highlight the cell or cells you want to move, then click and hold the left mouse button on the cells. Finally, move the cursor and the outline of the cells to the new location.

Spreadsheets Functions

New	**Create a New File**	Click **New** to create a new, blank document. When you first open the **Spreadsheets** application, a new, blank document is created for you.
Open	**Open Existing File**	Click **Open** to open an existing document. The **File Browser** window appears to help you find a document to open. If the document you want to open is in a folder, click the folder name to open the folder and list its contents. Once you find the document you want to open, click the name of the document, then click **Open**.
Save	**Save a Document**	Click **Save** to save the current document. The **File Browser** window appears the first time you save a file to help you find a place to store the new document. It's a good idea to save your document periodically - even if you are not finished.

Go Back to More — Click Back to close the Spreadsheet application and go back to the Moore page of applications.

 Print a Document — Click to print the current document. You'll need to have a printer turned on and connected to your computer. For more help with printers, click **Settings**, **Printer Settings**, then click **Help**.

 Select a Sheet — When creating a spreadsheet file, you start with three blank sheets - Sheet1, Sheet2, and Sheet3. You can switch between these sheets by using the **Sheet Selection** drop down menu, located on the left-hand side of the very top row. To choose a different sheet, click the button and select the sheet you wish to switch to.

When saving files, folders can be used to help organize your files. The New Folder button in the file browser allows you to create a new folder. To create a new folder, click New Folder, type a name for your folder, click Ok and you'll see your new folder. To store a file in that folder, click the folder name, click Open to open the folder, then then click Save to save the file in that folder.

Toolbar Buttons

At the top of the Spreadsheets application is a toolbar with buttons that provide helpful functions. Click the buttons in the toolbar to create different text effects or format your document. It's fun to experiment so be creative! Don't worry about remembering them all though because, if you forget what a button does, you can bring up a **Tool Tip** by placing the mouse cursor on top of the button. Below is a list of toolbar buttons.

 Font Type — Drop down menu to display a list of font types. Select the font you like, and the text you type will be in that font.

 Font Size — Drop down menu to display a list of font sizes. Select a size you like, and the text you type will be in that size.

 Font Color — Click the **Font Color** button to display a list of font colors. Select a color you like, and the text you type will be in that color.

Cell Color — Click the **Cell Color** button to display a list of cell colors. Select a color that you like, and the cell will appear in that color.

 Bold — Creates **bold text**.

Italic — Creates italic text.

Underline		Creates underlined text.
Horizontal Alignment		Dropdown to select horizontal alignment. See options below.
Align Left		Creates text aligned with the left margin of the cell.
Align Center		Creates text that is centered between the side margins of the cell.
Align Right		Creates text that is aligned with the right margin of the cell.
Justified		Fills gaps between the words so that the text fits evenly between the margins. Similar to a newspaper column.
Vertical Alignment		Drop down to select the vertical alignment of the cell. See options below.
Top		Creates text aligned with the upper margin of the cell.
Center		Creates text that is centered between the top and bottom margins of the cell.
Bottom		Creates text aligned with the lower margin of the cell. Default.
Number Format		Drop Down to select the format of numbers. See options below.
	General	This format leaves the number exactly the same as it is entered.
	1,234.00	This format gives displays two decimal places and inserts commas where needed.
	1,234	This format rounds up to the nearest whole number and inserts commas where needed.
	$1,234.00	This format displays the value in the form of US currency and inserts commas where needed.
	$1,234	This format displays the value rounded up to the nearest US dollar and inserts commas where needed
	1,234.00%	This format displays the value as a percent with two decimal places and inserts commas where needed
	1,234%	This format displays the value as a percent rounded to the nearest whole number. and inserts commas where needed

	DD/MM/YY	This format displays the value as a date in the form of day/month/year.
	MM/DD/YY	This format displays the value as a date in the form of month/day/year.
⊞	**Borders**	Located next to the Number Format drop down menu is the Borders button. Clicking this button will open a popup menu that allows you to put a border around one or more highlighted cells. Click a cell or highlight a group of cells, then Choose a border format or click advanced for more options.
f0	**Formulas**	Clicking the Formulas button will open a popup menu so that you may choose from a variety of mathematical functions. The popup menu will provide a list of all the functions as well as a brief description of each and how to use them.
Σ	**Auto Sum**	Highlight a group of cells in a single column or row; then click the button. This automatically adds the values of all the highlighted cells and puts the result in the next available cell in that column or row.
=	**Equals**	This button allows you to edit formulas in the **Cell Text Field**.
⊕ Insert	**Insert**	This button lets you add individual cells and entire rows or columns to your current sheet.
⊖ Delete	**Delete**	This button lets you remove individual cells and entire rows or columns from you current sheet.
Merge	**Merge**	This button lets you combine multiple cells into a single cell. If you click a cell that has been merged then this button will change to an unmerge button. Clicking unmerge will return the previously merged cell into multiple smaller cells.
	Cell Text Field	The white rectangle next to the equals sign is called the **Cell Text Field**. Here you can edit the text or formula that is in the cell you have selected.

Using Advanced Border Options:

1. Choose a color for your border from the color drop down menu.
2. Choose a line style for your border from one of the four style options located below
3. Select one or more lines that you want to add to your border with the color and style selections you have just made.

4. You can select different colors and styles for different lines to add or change current lines by repeating the previous steps.
5. A preview of your border is on the rightmost side of the popup window. If at any time you wish to start over you can click the **Clear** button located below the preview.
6. When you are done editing your border click **OK** to apply the border or **Cancel** to return to your spreadsheet without applying your border.

Quick Stats

At the bottom of the screen just above the slider are three *Quick Stats*: **Sum**, **Average**, and **Count**.

Sum

This number represents the total of the values of all highlighted cells. If a cell contains a non-numerical value, it will not be added to the sum.

Average

This number represents the average of all highlighted cells. If a cell contains a non-numerical value, it will not be included in the average. For example, if the cells highlighted contained: 7, 0, 11, a, and 2 then average would equal to $7 + 0 + 11 + 2 = 20 / 4 = 5$.

Count

This number counts how many cells are highlighted. If a cell is blank it will not be counted.

Stopwatch

This is a stopwatch application that you can use to record the duration of an event.

To use the Stopwatch:
- **Click the More button**
- **Click the Stopwatch icon**

Stopwatch Functions

Go

Click Go to start or resume the stopwatch. The button will change to read **Pause**.

Pause

Click Pause to stop a stopwatch.

Reset

Click Reset to set your stopwatch back to zero.

Using Multiple Stopwatches

Add Stopwatch

To create a new stopwatch, click **Add Stopwatch**. You can add up to four stopwatches at the same time.

Remove Stopwatch

Clicking **Remove Stopwatch** will remove the last stopwatch that you added.

 # Timer

This application contains a number of timers that you can use to set various alarms for.

The following instructions assume that you have:
- **Clicked on the More button**
- **Clicked on the Timer icon**

Using Timers

Set a Timer

You may create several timers. Follow these instructions to set a timer:

1. Use the arrow keys to set the amount of time you would like to count down from.
2. Enter a name for the timer using the **Name** field if you wish.
3. Click **Go** to start or resume the timer. The button will then change to a **Pause** button. Click **Pause** to stop the timer.

Reset a Timer

If a timer is paused or has run down to zero, then clicking **Reset** will set the timer to the previous set time. Clicking **Reset** before the timer is set will set the timer to the default time of **two minutes**.

Add a Timer

To create a new timer, click **Add Timer**

NOTE: You can set a maximum of 4 timers at once.

Remove a Timer

To remove the last timer added, click **Remove Timer**

 # Write

This application allows you to create, edit, and view documents with a simple, easy-to-use word processor.

To use the Write application:

- **Click the More button**
- **Click the Write icon**

Write Functions

 Create a New File Click New to create a new, blank document. When you first open the Write application, a new, blank document is created for you.

 Open Existing File Click Open to open an existing document. The File Browser window appears to help you find a document to open. If the document you want to open is in a folder, click the folder name to open the folder and list its contents. Once you find the document you want to open, click the name of the document, then click Open.

 Save a Document Click **Save** to save the current document. The *File Browser* window appears the first time you save a document to help you find a place to store the new document. Click the white text field next to the word **Name**, then type a name for your document. After you have chosen a name for your document, click the green **Save** button. It's a good idea to save your document periodically - even if you are not finished.

If you have already saved your document, you can also save it under a new name by pressing the **Save As** button, changing the file name, and pressing the **Save** button. Saving a document under a new name saves it as a new file and so leaves the original unchanged.

When saving documents, folders can be used to help organize your documents. The *New Folder* button in the file browser allows you to create a new folder. To create a new folder, click *New Folder*, type a name for your folder, click **Ok** and you'll see your new folder. To store a document in that folder, click the folder name, click **Open** to open the folder, then click **Save** to save the document in that folder.

 Go Back to More Click Back to close the Write application and go back to the Moore page of applications.

 Print a Document Click to print the current document. You'll need to have a printer turned on and connected to your computer. For more help with printers, click Settings,

Printer Settings, then click Help.

If you have already saved your document, you can also save it under a new name by pressing the **Save As** button, changing the file name, and pressing the **Save** button. Saving a document under a new name saves it as a new file and so leaves the original unchanged.

When saving documents, folders can be used to help organize your documents. The **New Folder** button in the file browser allows you to create a new folder. To create a new folder, click **New Folder**, type a name for your folder, click **Ok** and you'll see your new folder. To store a document in that folder, click the folder name, click **Open** to open the folder, then then click **Save** to save the document in that folder.

Keyboard Controls

Functions like **Cut**, **Copy**, and **Paste** can be utilized by using a combination of keystrokes from your keyboard. To Cut or Copy, simply highlight the text you wish to duplicate, then:

- To Copy, press and hold down the **ctrl** key with one finger, tap the "C" key once and release the **ctrl** key.
- To Cut, press and hold down the **ctrl** key with one finger, tap the "X" key once and release the **ctrl** key.

To **Paste** text that you have copied or cut, simply click where you would like to place the text, then:

- Press and hold down the **ctrl** key with one finger, tap the "V" key once and release the **ctrl** key.

NOTE: Keyboard Controls will only work a real keyboard; the on-screen keyboard will not work.

Toolbar Buttons

At the top of the **Write** application is a toolbar with buttons that provide helpful functions. Click the buttons in the toolbar to create different text effects or format your document. It's fun to experiment so be creative! Below is a list of toolbar buttons.

Button	Name	Description
▼	Font Type	Drop down menu to display a list of font types. Select the font you like, and the text you type will be in that font.
14 ▼	Font Size	Drop down menu to display a list of font sizes. Select a size you like, and the text you type will be in that size.
A	Font Color	Click the **Font Color** button to display a list of font colors. Select a color you like, and the text you type will be in that color.
☐	Cell Color	Click the **Cell Color** button to display a list of cell colors. Select a color that you like, and the cell will appear in that color.
B	Bold	Creates **bold text**.

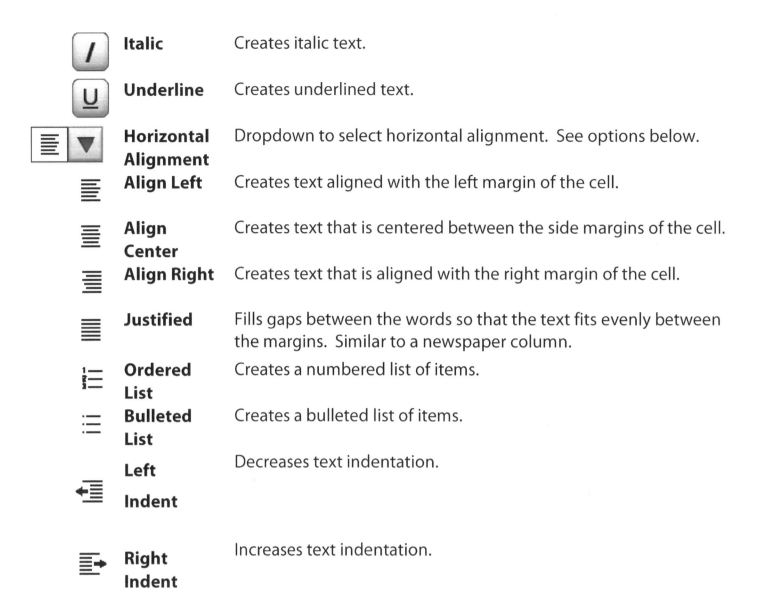

I	**Italic**	Creates italic text.
U	**Underline**	Creates underlined text.
	Horizontal Alignment	Dropdown to select horizontal alignment. See options below.
	Align Left	Creates text aligned with the left margin of the cell.
	Align Center	Creates text that is centered between the side margins of the cell.
	Align Right	Creates text that is aligned with the right margin of the cell.
	Justified	Fills gaps between the words so that the text fits evenly between the margins. Similar to a newspaper column.
	Ordered List	Creates a numbered list of items.
	Bulleted List	Creates a bulleted list of items.
	Left Indent	Decreases text indentation.
	Right Indent	Increases text indentation.

Spell Check

When you are writing a document, you might notice that occasionally words are underlined with a jagged red line. This means that these words may be misspelled. You can right-click the underlined word to see possible corrections. Please be aware that the red line does not necessarily mean that a word IS misspelled but rather that it is not recognized by the computer. A common example of this is a person's last name.

My Profile Settings

To view your Profile…
- **Click on the Home button**
- **Click on the Settings button (located in the upper right corner of the screen)**
- **Click on My Profile**

Enter Profile Information

Click in the space next to any of the following fields to enter or update your profile information. When you are finished, click **Save Changes**. If you do not want to keep the change(s), click **Cancel Changes**.

First Name - Enter your first name in this field.

Last Name - Enter your last name in this field.

Phone Number - Enter your phone number in this field.

Address 1, 2, and 3 - Enter your street address in these fields.

City - Enter the name of your city in this field.

State/Province - Enter the name of your state or province in this field.

Zip Code - Enter your zip code in this field. This updates the **Weather** location.

Birthday - Click each of the droplists to select the day, month, and year.

Anniversary - Click the droplists to select the day, month, and year of your anniversary.

Profile Picture

Click **Change Picture** to change your default profile picture. A popup window will open to allow you to choose a photo from one of your albums. Click the album containing the photo you want for your profile, click the photo, and then click **OK**. Alternatively, you can take a picture of yourself using the built-in camera by following these instructions:

1. Click the **Use Camera** button.
2. A small preview window will appear. Use this window to decide how you want to appear in your photo.
3. When you are ready to take the picture, click the green **Take Picture** button, located above the preview window.
4. Upon clicking the Take picture button, a count down from 3 will begin and then your picture will be taken.
5. If you are satisfied with the photo, click **Done**. If not, simply reposition yourself and start over from step 3.

User Accounts

This page lets you configure and manage the user accounts for your computer.

The following instructions assume that you have:
- **Clicked on the Home button**
- **Clicked on the Settings button (located in the upper right corner of the screen)**
- **Clicked on Users**

A user account is a way to control access to your computer. If you create a user account, you can lock your computer by logging out. You will also be asked to login to your computer each time you turn it on. To get more help on how to login/logout, click the Home button, and then click **Help**.

Here are some examples of scenarios where user accounts are useful:

- Two members of the household each have their own email account and want to use the same computer, but access their email accounts separately. Two user accounts would be created; one for each person.
- Guests are coming over and you want them to be able to use the internet on your computer, but don't want them to see your email - or other important data on your computer. One user account would be created, and you would log out of your account when you have visitors, putting the computer into Guest Mode.

If you are the only person using your computer and/or do not need to protect your data, then you most likely do not need to create a user account.

Types of Accounts

You can create up to three user accounts on your computer. There are two different kinds of user accounts that can be created:

- Primary Account - your computer can only have one primary user account. The person logged into the primary user account can create and manage secondary accounts. A primary user account must be created before any secondary user accounts can be created.
- Secondary Account - your computer can have up to two additional secondary accounts. The person logged into a secondary user account can only manage their own account.

Guest Mode

Once you create a user account, you can easily put your computer into Guest Mode by logging out of your account. Guest mode will disable certain features of your computer, while allowing access to the internet via the Web button. The following features will be disabled while in Guest Mode:

- Video Chat
- Email
- Photos
- Calendar
- Contacts

Managing Accounts

Create a Primary User Account

The first user account you create is the called the primary user account. All other accounts created are called secondary accounts. A primary user account must be created before any secondary user accounts can be created.

As the primary user, you will be able to create and manage secondary (other) user accounts. Secondary users can only manage their own accounts.

To create the primary account, please do the following:

1. Click **Settings**. If you were on the **Home** page, skip to step 3.
2. Click **General Settings**.
3. Click **Users**
4. Enter the desired username in the **Current User:** field. Here are the rules for creating a username:
    - must be 8-45 characters long
    - must start with a letter
    - must be only letters and numbers
    - must not contain spaces
1. Optional: A password is not required. If you want to create a password for your account, then enter your desired password in the **Password:** and **Verify Password** fields. Here are the rules for creating a password.
    - is case sensitive (capital letters and small letters matter)
    - must be 8-16 characters
    - must not contain spaces
    - must contain at least one UPPER CASE letter
    - must contain at least one number
2. Optional: Choose one or two security questions and enter the answers. You will be asked the security questions if you forget your password.
3. Click **Save**
4. Write down the username and password (if you have created one) for the primary account

If you have a password set up for your account and have the screen lock enabled, it is recommended that you set up two security questions that you can answer, so you can login if you forget your password.

Create a Secondary User Account

Only the primary user may create secondary accounts. To create a secondary account, you must be logged into the primary user account. Once logged in, please do the following:

1. Click **Settings**. If you were on the Home page, skip to step 3.
2. Click **General Settings**
3. Click **Users**
4. Click **Add User**

5. Enter the desired username in the **Username:** field. Here are the rules for creating a username:
    - must be 8-45 characters long
    - must start with a letter
    - must be only letters and numbers
    - must not contain spaces
6. Optional: A password is not required. If you want to create a password for your account, then enter your desired password in the **Password:** and **Verify Password** fields. Here are the rules for creating a password.
    - is case sensitive (capital letters and small letters matter)
    - must be 8-16 characters
    - must not contain spaces
    - must contain at least one UPPER CASE letter
    - must contain at least one number
7. Click **Save**
8. Write down the username and password (if you have created one) for the secondary account

Once the secondary user account is created, the person can log into their account and enter their security questions; however it is completely optional.

Delete a Secondary User Account

You must be logged in to the primary user account to delete secondary user accounts. To delete a secondary user account, please do the following:

1. Click **Settings**. If you were on the Home page, skip to step 3
2. Click **General Settings**
3. Click **Users**
4. From the **Manage User** droplist, select the user you want to delete
5. Click **Remove User**.
6. When the dialog box will appear saying, "Are you sure you wish to remove this user", click **Yes**.

Change Account Username/Password/Questions

When you are logged in, you can change your username, password and/or security questions at any time.

If you have a password set up for your account and have the **screen lock** enabled, it is recommended that you set up two security questions that you can answer, so you can login if you forget your password.

To make changes to your user account, please do the following:
1. Click Settings. If you were on the Home page, skip to step 3.
2. Click General Settings
3. Click Users - your account information will appear at the top of the screen
4. You may change your username, password and/or security questions, and then click Save to save your changes

If you are logged into the primary user account, you can only change the username and/or password for secondary accounts. The secondary user can create/change their security questions by logging into their user account, then following the instructions to Change Account Username/Password/Questions. To change the username/password for a secondary account, please do the following:
1. Click Settings. If you were on the Home page, skip to step 3.
2. Click General Settings
3. Click Users
4. From the Manage User droplist, select the user you want to edit
5. You may change the username/password, and then click Save to save your change

Video Chat Settings

To log into or log out of Video Chat:
- **Click the Video Chat button**
- **Click the Settings button (located in the upper right corner of the screen)**

This page allows you to configure your computer with your Skype™ account username and password in order to use the Video Chat application.

Enter Skype Account

A Skype™ account consists of a username and password.

If you have a Skype™ account, enter your username and password in the fields provided and click Save Changes to log into Skype™. The computer will attempt to log into your account. If successful, you will see the status, "Logged In". If your account is not logged in - or if there is a problem logging in, you will see the status "Logged Out".

Create Skype Account

If you do not have a Skype™ account and want to create one, you may create one easily from this page. To create your Skype™ account, follow these instructions:
1. Click Video Chat.
2. Click Settings.
3. Click New Account.

4. Enter a username of your choosing in the first text field. Here are the rules for creating a username:
    - must be 6-32 characters long
    - must start with a letter
    - must be only letters and numbers
    - must not contain spaces
    - can have period '.', dash '-', underscore "_' or comma ','
5. Enter a password of your choosing in the second text field then retype it in the third text field. Here are the rules for creating a password:
    - is case sensitive (capital letters and small letters matter)
    - must be 6-20 characters
    - must not contain spaces
    - must contain at least one letter
    - must contain at least one number
6. Click the check box below the third text field to indicate your acceptance of the Skype™ License Agreement. If you wish to read the Skype™ License Agreement, click the **License** button to the left of the **Create Account** button.
7. Click Create Account. Please be aware that the name you choose may already be taken and it may take several attempts to create a unique account.
8. Click Save Changes. This will log you in to your new Skype™ account.
9. Write down your username and password and keep it in a safe place.
10. Follow the steps above in "Enter Skype Account" to enter your new Skype account username and password.

Email Settings

The following instructions assume that you have:
- **Click the Email button**
- **Click the Settings button (located in the upper right corner of the screen)**

This page allows you to enter your email account credentials and settings in order to use the Email application. It is comprised of three sections, Account, Folders and Options that you can navigate between, using the buttons located on the right-hand side

Email Account Setup

Email Address/Password

An email account has an email address and password. An example of an email address is Cutie@GreenCity.com. Another example is WhiteKnight10@FireLight.net.

To configure your computer with your email account, enter your email address and the password into the provided fields and then click Save. The computer will attempt to connect to the email server. Upon successful connection, you will see **Email Account Status: Connected**.

Removing an Email Address

If you ever want to change or remove the email address that you have set up on your computer, click the Remove Account button. This will delete your email settings and all the email sent to this account. You may then enter a different email address if you wish.

Advanced Account Options

NOTE: Do not check the Show advanced options box unless you are familiar with advanced email protocol or unless instructed to do so by a trusted Tech Buddy or Customer Support. If you have changed settings unintentionally, click Reset to Defaults in order to reset your email settings to the default information.

The values for your email account settings are provided by your email host. If you are unsure of your email settings, you should contact your email host.

Protocol

Use the droplist to select IMAP or POP3 email protocol. IMAP synchronizes your emails with the server (e.g., deleting emails on your computer will also delete them on the server). POP3 only downloads your emails to your computer. If your email host supports POP, and you select this option, it is advisable to check the Leave Messages on Server checkbox to leave a copy of your email messages on the server. Not all protocols may be supported by your email host.

Incoming Security

Use the droplist to select incoming mail security: TLS (Transport Layer Security), SSL (Secure Sockets Layer), or None.

Incoming Mail Server

The incoming mail server is the web address of the server used to transport email to your computer.

Incoming Server Port

The incoming mail server port is the computer port used to communicate with the incoming mail server.

Incoming Username

The incoming username is used by some hosts when logging into the incoming mail server. It may be the same as your email address - or just the part before the "@".

Outgoing Security

Use the droplist to select outgoing mail security: **TLS** (Transport Layer Security), **SSL** (Secure Sockets Layer), or **None**.

Outgoing Mail Server

The outgoing mail server is the web address of the server used to transport email from your computer.

Outgoing Server Port

The outgoing mail server port is the computer port used to communicate with the outgoing mail server.

Outgoing Username

The outgoing username is used by some hosts when logging into the outgoing mail server. It may be the same as your email address - or just the part before the "@".

Outgoing Password

The outgoing password is used by some hosts in conjunction with the outgoing username when logging into the outgoing mail server.

If you are having trouble setting up your email account and need further assistance, please call Customer Support.

Email Folder Settings

Existing Folders List

This page displays a list of all of your folders and allows you to manage your *Inbox* folder list.

NOTE: Some folders are integral to your email and cannot be moved, renamed or deleted. You will receive a warning if you attempt to do so.

Add

This button lets you create new folders in which to store and organize your email. To create a new folder, follow these instructions:

1. Click **Add**.
2. A dialog box will appear asking you to enter a name for your new folder. Type a name in the text box, but be aware that it cannot be the same as an existing folder.
3. Click **OK** to create your new folder; however if you change your mind and no longer wish to create a folder, click **Cancel**.

Rename

This button lets you change the name of an existing folder. To rename an existing folder, follow these instructions:

1. Click the check box next to the folder you want to rename.
2. Click **Rename**.

3. A dialog box will appear asking you to enter a new name for your folder. Type a name in the text box, but be aware that it cannot be the same as an existing folder.
4. Click **OK** to rename your folder; however if you change your mind and no longer wish to rename this folder, click **Cancel**.

Remove

This button lets you delete a folder. To remove an existing folder, follow these instructions:

1. Click the check box next to the folder you want to remove
2. Click *Remove*
3. You will be asked to confirm your decision. Click *Yes* to delete the folder, or *Cancel* to cancel the operation

Move Up

This button lets you move the selected folder up in the **Inbox** folder list. To move a folder up, follow these instructions:

1. Click in the checkbox next to the folder you want to move up
2. Click **Move Up**

You will see the folder moved up one item in the list on the settings page. The changes will be reflected in the **Inbox** folder list. Tip: Put folders that you use most at the top.

Move Down

This button lets you move the selected folder down in the **Inbox** folder list. To move a folder down, follow these instructions:

1. Click in the checkbox next to the folder you want to move down
2. Click **Move Down**

You will see the folder moved down one item in the list on the settings page. The changes will be reflected in the **Inbox** folder list. Tip: Put folders that you use least at the bottom.

Email Options

Compose Options

This option allows you to show either the **CC** or **BCC** field while composing emails. These fields are used to organize your email recipients. CC stands for "Carbon Copy" and **BCC** stands for "Blind Carbon Copy". These terms originally applied to paper correspondence and now also apply to email.

Show CC

Selecting this option will show the **CC** field and hide the **BCC** field. CC refers to the practice of sending a message to multiple recipients where the recipients are organized into primary and secondary recipients. Primary recipients are entered into the **To** field and secondary recipients are entered into the **CC** field. Email recipients entered into the **CC** field will receive a copy of the email and their email addresses will be visible to all recipients of the email.

Show BCC

Selecting this option will hide the CC field and show the BCC field. BCC refers to the practice of sending a message to multiple recipients in a way that conceals some of the recipients. Email recipients entered into the BCC field will receive a copy of the email; however, their email addresses will be concealed from all other recipients.

Facebook Settings

This function keeps track of your connection to Facebook

The following instructions assume that you have:
- **Click the Photos button**
- **Click the Settings button (located in the upper right corner of the screen)**

This page allows you to enter your Facebook account credentials in order to use the photo sharing feature of the Photos application.

Facebook Connection

Your computer allows you to connect directly to Facebook using your Facebook log-in and password. This computer uses Facebook to automatically add friends to your Address Book and friend's pictures to your Photos application.

If you have a Facebook account, log in one time and your settings will be saved for future use. You will see the words **"Already Logged In"** at the bottom of the page if you are successfully connected to Facebook. If you do not have a Facebook account, select the main Web app to go to Facebook's home page (www.Facebook.com) and create an account, then return to this page.

Refresh

Select this button to refresh your Facebook page and you will see any new updates that your friends have posted such as photos or contact info changes.

Log Out

You may log out of Facebook at any time by selecting this button.

System Info

This page lets you view status information about your computer.

To view your System Information:
- **Click the Home button**
- **Click the Settings button (located in the upper right corner of the screen)**
- **Click the System Info button**

Status information

This section displays basic information about the services to which your computer connects, including information such as the network connection status and status of any accounts you have configured.

A connected icon: ✓ indicates an account is logged in - or a good connection.

A disconnected icon: ✗ indicates that an account may not be configured - or that there may be a problem with this setting.

Get VIP Backup and Support

If you are not subscribed to VIP Backup and Support then the **Get VIP Backup and Support** button will appear. Clicking this button will cause a popup to appear where you can subscribe to this fee-based, monthly service. The benefits of VIP Backup and Support are:

1. Priority Calling: When you call our customer support line, your calls will be answered more quickly and with higher priority.
2. Network Backup: Your data is backed up to our servers safely and securely.
3. Remote Access Support: We can connect to your computer and see what you see in order to provide support and tutorials.

Update

The Update button is used to initiate a manual software update. You may be asked by Customer Service to click this button. Your computer will automatically check for updated software, so you will normally not need to click this button. Remember, all software updates are free!

Restart

The Restart button is used to restart your computer. Clicking Restart will reboot your computer and use any new software that was downloaded to your computer during your last session.

System information

Below the status information, you will see information about your computer. This section is mostly useful to Customer Support, specifically, the Device ID and User ID.

System messages

At the bottom of the page, is a blank area that is used to display system messages from your computer. If you initiate a software update by clicking the Update button, you will see the system message, "Manual Software Update Started" and the date and time. Similarly, when a software update has been installed, this message will be displayed: "New software has been installed". This section will usually remain empty. If you receive a system message, a notice will appear in the Notices section of the Home screen. Clicking the notice will take you to this page to view the system message.

System Settings

This page lets you adjust personalized settings for your computer.

The following instructions assume that you have:
- **Click the Home button**
- **Click the Settings button (located in the upper right corner of the screen)**
- **Click the System Settings button**

System Settings

Time Zone

Click the droplist ▼ to select your local time zone.

Set Time

The time on your computer will be automatically set whenever you are connected to the internet; however if you are not connected to the internet, a **Set Time** button will appear and allow you to set the time manually.

Use Built-in Speakers

Check this box: ✓ to enable or disable the use of the built-in speakers.

Disabling this check box will deactivate the internal speakers so that you can plug in external speakers or headphones, while enabling the check box will reactivate the built-in speakers.

Use External Microphone

Check this box: ✓ to enable or disable the use of an external microphone.

There should already be an external microphone connected to your computer when you first receive it and this setting should be checked.

Calibrate Touchscreen

Click **Calibrate Touchscreen**, to adjust the calibration of your touch screen. You will be presented with highlighted targets on your screen that you must touch, one by one – press down for at least two seconds on each target for the computer to register your touch. At the completion of the calibration, your computer will be automatically restarted.

Cursor Color / Cursor Size

To adjust the appearance of your mouse pointer, use the provided droplists to select mouse color and mouse size.

NOTE: You will need to restart the computer to see the changes. To restart, click System Info and click the Restart button.

Screen Saver

Use the droplist ▼ to choose a screen saver. You can choose from a slideshow of your favorite photos or a blank screen that will read "Touch Here!". If you do not want a screen saver, select **None**.

NOTE: The touchscreen on this computer does not experience "burn-in" and a screen saver is not required.

Idle Time

This is the period of inactivity that occurs before the screen saver you have selected will begin. Use the droplist ▼ to select an idle time from 2 **minutes** up to **2 hours**.

Enable Screen Lock

Checking this box will require you to enter your password before you can use your computer after a screen saver has started. This setting will be disabled if you have not set a password on your account.

Automatic Logout

Checking this box will cause your computer to automatically log you out if your computer is idle for the amount of time that you select from the droplist. The time amounts that you can choose from are:

- Five Minutes
- Ten Minutes
- Fifteen Minutes

Print Settings

This page allows you to view and configure printers and print requests.

To view the Printer Settings
- **Click the Home button**
- **Click the Settings button (located in the upper right corner of the screen)**
- **Click the Print Settings Button**

Printers

Currently, the computer supports many printers from Hewlett Packard (HP). The printer must be connected directly to the computer with a USB printer cable. If the printer has memory card slots, you will be able to view and download photos just like you can with cards connected directly to the computer. If the printer has a scanning feature, you will be able to scan pictures into the computer. The *Scanner* application is available in the *More* section. At this time, faxing is not supported through the computer. You may fax directly from the printer.

Note: At this time the faxing feature of all-in-one printers is not supported. Faxing may be done directly through the printer.

USB Connections

The printer must be connected directly to the computer with a USB printer (A/B) cable. The rectangular end of the cable, which looks like those on the keyboard and mouse, should be plugged into any USB connector on the left side of the computer. The square end of the cable plugs into the printer, usually in the back.

Recommended Models

The following printers have been tested for compatibility with your computer

- HP Deskjet 1000
- HP Photosmart 5510
- HP Photosmart 7510
- HP Deskjet D2860
- HP Officejet 4500
- HP Officejet 6500A Plus
- HP Officejet Pro 8600 Plus

Supported Printers

If you would like to see if your printer is compatible with your computer, enter this URL into your browser address bar and click GO: http://hplipopensource.com/hplip-web/supported_devices/index.html. Then follow these instructions:

1. Select the type of printer you have from the first drop down menu.
2. Select your printer's model from the second drop down menu.
3. Click the **Continue** button.
4. Check the first table next to the words **Minimum HPLIP version**. If you see the version number **3.12.4** or earlier then continue to step 5. If not then your printer is not compatible with your computer.
5. Check the first table next to the words **Support level**. If you see the word **Full** then continue to step 6. If not then your printer is not compatible with your computer.
6. Check the first table next to the word **Recommended?** If you see the word **Yes** then continue to step 7; otherwise your printer is not compatible with your computer.
7. Check the second table next to the words **USB I/O**. If you see the word **Yes** then continue to step 8; otherwise your printer is not compatible with your computer.
8. Check the last table next to the words **Driver plug-in**. If you see the word **None** then continue to step 9; otherwise your printer is not compatible with your computer.
9. Check the last table next to the words **Requires firmware download**. If you see the word **No** then your printer is compatible with your computer; otherwise your printer is not compatible with your computer.

Printer Information

Printer Name

On the left side of the screen, you will see the name of any printer that was connected to the computer's USB port and powered on. If you just connected a printer, it could take a minute before the printer appears.

Print Test Page

This button will appear whenever your printer is ready to print. Clicking this button will print out a letter sized page after a short delay. Use this to verify your computer is talking to the printer and your printer is functioning normally.

Printer Status

On the right side of the screen, you will see the printer's current status. A change in the status may not appear immediately.

Printer is Ready

This indicates the printer is ready for printing and not currently printing anything.

Printer Not Ready

This indicates the printer is not ready for printing. There are several things you can check to fix this problem:

- The printer is turned on.
- The USB printer cable is plugged in to both the printer and computer.
- The paper is loaded into the printer.
- There are no errors on the printer. Errors may be shown on its display or indicated by a red or flashing light. Please follow the instructions on the display or consult the printer's User Manual to clear any error conditions.

Working on 1 Print Request

This will appear if you had recently tried printing something and it has not finished printing yet. It may also appear if you had been printing something and the printer was turned off or disconnected from the computer before printing was complete. A number greater than one (1) indicates you started to print a second item before the first item completed printing. It is ok to continue to use the computer while your items are being printed.

Cancel Print Request

This button will appear if you have one or more print requests being worked on. Clicking the button will cancel the oldest print request being worked on.

You may want to cancel a print request if it does not look the way you expected. You may also want to cancel a print request if it had been canceled at the printer first, or the printer was disconnected or turned off during printing.

If the printer was disconnected or turned off, cancel before re-connecting or turning on the printer. Otherwise, the printer may start printing immediately or print incorrectly.

NOTE: Any information that has already been sent to the printer will continue to print. Please use the printer's cancel *button to cancel printing anything that had already been sent to the printer. If there were any problems performing the cancel, the next item may not print correctly.*

Print Request Settings

This is the popup that appears when you want to print. This allows you to choose a few printing options.

Page Orientation

On the left-hand side of this popup are the **Page Orientation** checkboxes. These checkboxes are **Portrait**, which means that the vertical edge is longer than the horizontal edge, and **Landscape**, which means that the horizontal edge is longer than the vertical edge.

Copies

This field lets you choose how many times the page you are printing will be printed.

📶 Network Settings

This page allows you to connect to the Internet and view some of your network settings.

To view the Network Settings:
- Click the Home button
- Click the Settings button (located in the upper right corner of the screen)
- Click the Network Settings button

Network Interface Diagram

The diagram at the top of the screen shows how your computer is currently connected to the Internet. From left to right, it illustrates the connection from your computer to your modem or router, and then from your modem/router to the Internet. A successful connection from your computer to the Internet will display two green connected icons: . If at either point you see a red disconnected: ❌, then you are having a problem connecting to your network.

The Test Network button will display the speeds at which information is being sent back and forth between your computer and the Internet, and also the strength of your wireless network if you are connected to a wireless network (WiFi).

IP address

You will also notice a string of numbers (ex. 192.168.1.1) below the picture of the computer. This is known as an **IP address**. It will only display when your computer is successfully connected to a network. Lack of an IP address can be an indicator of a possible problem connecting to the Internet. This number can change over time.

Network Interfaces

Below the network interface diagram, you will see two tables that represent the two interfaces that can be used to connect to the Internet, **Wired Network** and **Wireless Network(s)**.

Wired Network

To connect to a wired network, you will need an Ethernet cable. You should have received one with your computer. This cable is similar to a phone cable, but the connector is wider. Like a phone cable, there is a little plastic tab that should click when plugged in. The plastic tab also needs to be pressed to remove the cable. If the tab is broken or missing, the cable will not stay in reliably.

Connecting this cable is simple. One end of the cable plugs in to the network port at the back of your computer. To locate the network port, refer to the **Quick Start Guide** that came with the computer. The other end of the cable plugs into the modem provided by your Internet provider, or, if you are using one, a router. The modem/router may have multiple ports. Any of the empty ports marked as wired, Ethernet, local, or LAN (Local Area Network) can be used. **DO NOT** use the single port marked Internet or modem. This single port is for use by your Internet provider. If you received two boxes from your Internet provider, use the box that is not connected directly to the wall.

Wireless Network(s)

Your computer is enabled to use a wireless (WiFi) network. If you would like to use WiFi, you will need to either have or purchase a wireless router at your local electronics store. Alternately, the modem provided by your Internet Provider may be configured to be a wireless network. In the **Wireless Network(s)** table, you will see all of the wireless networks that are available to your computer.

Understanding the Network Interface Tables

Both the **Wired Network** and **Wireless Network(s)** tables contain multiple columns of information to help you easily see information about that network.

Network name

The first column in each table displays the **Name** of the network. Only those with the strongest signals are shown. This information updates periodically.

MAC Address

This address uniquely identifies the box given to you by your Internet Provider. If multiple networks have the same name, this address can be used to determine which is yours. The address may appear on the side or bottom of the box.

Security Type (wireless only)

Your computer supports the following security types in order from strongest to weakest: WPA2/AES, WPA/TKIP, WEP, and None. Variations of these types, such as WEP64, are also supported. The security should have been set by your Internet provider and may be indicated on the side or bottom of the box.

Signal Strength (wireless only)

Many things affect the signal strength of a wireless network and the strength will fluctuate. Your neighbor's network could actually appear stronger. If you try changing anything to improve the signal strength, you must keep it that way for a minute to see whether it made things better or worse.

- Walls and furniture between the computer and the box given to you from your Internet provider can reduce the signal strength. Try to have a clear line of sight between them.
- The box given to you by your Internet provider has an internal or external antenna. Try pointing the antenna in different directions, rotating the box, or laying the box on its side.
- Cordless phones can have an adverse effect on your signal. Don't have a cordless phone right next to your Internet provider's box or the computer.

Status

The last column in each table displays the connection status for that network interface. You can have both types of interfaces connected at the same time, but the **wired** connection is generally faster and will be chosen automatically if both types are available.

The currently connected networks in either table will display a green connected icon: .

Connecting Wirelessly

In the **Status** column of the **Wireless Network(s)** table, you will notice **Connect** buttons that allow you to connect to any of the wireless networks available to your computer. You can only be connected to one wireless network at a time.

Connect to your Wireless Network

1. Determine which of the networks shown is your network. Your wireless network name should have been given to you by your Internet Provider. It may also be written on the side or bottom of the box given to you by your Internet provider. In most cases, your home network should appear at the top of the list since it will most likely have the strongest signal.
2. Click the **Connect** button next to your network.
3. A pop-up window will appear showing you the network's information. You will be asked for any additional information if it is needed.
4. Click **Ok**.

NOTE: It could take several minutes to connect to a wireless network.

Passwords

A password may also be called passphrase or key. Sometimes, the name of a hidden network is also referred to as a password. If a password is needed, it should have been given to you by your Internet Provider. The password may also be written on the side or bottom of the box given to you by your Internet Provider. For the "WEP security type", it may be indicated as "WEP KEY" on the box.

Tech Buddy Settings

This page lets you create and manage a Tech Buddy.

To get to the Tech Buddy account page:
- **Click the Home button**
- **Click the Settings button**
- **Click the Tech Buddy button**

Tech Buddy is a great feature that allows a family member or trusted friend to provide you with remote assistance - from anywhere! When your Tech Buddy connects to your computer remotely, they'll be able to see your computer screen and control the mouse and keyboard. This can be very useful if you need a little extra guidance and/or are having difficulty describing what you're seeing on your computer.

To use the Tech Buddy feature, there are three basic steps:

1. Create a Tech Buddy Account - you will do this on your computer.
2. Install the Remote Access Software - your Tech Buddy will do this on their computer.
3. Run a Remote Session - your Tech Buddy will do this on their computer.

Since some of these steps must be performed by your Tech Buddy, it is advisable to print out this page and give it to them.

To print this page, click the **Print** button: .

Create a Tech Buddy Account

The Tech Buddy account will be used by your Tech Buddy. The account consists of a username, a password and an email address. You will create the account, and then give the information to your Tech Buddy.

To create a Tech Buddy account, follow these instructions:

1. Click **Settings**
2. Click **Tech Buddy**
3. Enter a username and a password

   Username Rules
   - Must not have any spaces
   - Must be between 8-16 characters

Password Rules
- Must not have any spaces
- Must be between 8-16 characters
- Must have at least one number
- Must have at least one uppercase letter
- Must be different than the username.

4. Enter your Tech Buddy's email address - this is NOT your email address
5. Click Save.

You will need to give your Tech Buddy the username and password that you just created.

Install the Remote Access Software

Your Tech Buddy will need the username and password in order to complete this step. Have your Tech Buddy follow these instructions to install the software:

1. Go to www.telikin.com.
2. Click the "Tech Buddy login" link in the top right corner of the screen.
3. Enter the Tech Buddy username and password and click "Log In".
4. **Windows:** click "Download Windows Tech Buddy", and follow the installation instructions.
5. **MAC:** select "Download MAC VNC Viewer", and follow the installation instructions.

Run a Remote Session

Once your Tech Buddy has installed the remote access software, have them follow these instructions to establish a remote connection to your computer:

Windows
1. Start the Tech Buddy Helper application.
2. Click Connect
3. Enter your Tech Buddy username and password.
4. Click Ok

The remote session will start and a window will open. The window will show you the machine you are connecting to and you can then use your mouse and keyboard to control it. To close the remote session, click the X in the top right corner of the window.

MAC
1. Start the Chicken of the VNC application.
2. Go to www.telikin.com; click the "Tech Buddy login" link in the top right corner of the screen.
3. Enter your Tech Buddy username and password and click "Log In".

4. Follow the instructions to get the **IP Address**, **Port Number** and **Session Password**...
5. Enter that information into Chicken of the VNC and connect.

The remote session will start and a window will open. The window will show you the machine you are connecting to and you can then use your mouse and keyboard to control it. To close the remote session, click the X in the top right corner of the window.

Allow Unacknowledged Support

By checking this box, your Tech Buddy will be able to remotely access your computer without your permission.

NOTE: Do not check this box unless your Tech Buddy is a trusted friend or family member.

Browser Settings

Browser settings let you choose what kind of websites to allow or filter out. If you are the Primary user you can regulate the web filter for guests and other users. Be aware that this will filter out most but not all websites in specific categories.

To view the Browser Settings:
- **Click the Web button**
- **Click the Settings button (located in the upper right corner of the screen)**

Web Settings

Default Zoom

This value is the default magnification setting for all your web pages. Try setting this value to 30%, then viewing your web pages to see if this is right for you. You may need to adjust this value to find a magnification that is right for you. The higher the value, the greater the magnification.

NOTE: If you are using magnification and are not seeing all content on a web page - or some items are hidden or not available - try setting your magnification to a lower setting. Some web pages do not work at higher magnifications. This is due to restrictions on the web page itself.

Enable Web Filter

This check box activates the web filter and lets you choose what to block. The options and descriptions are as follows:

- **Graphic Content** - This option blocks: adult content, art nudes, mixed adult, naturism/nudism, pornography, and sexuality.
- **Drugs and Alcohol** - This option blocks: beer & liquor information, beer & liquor sale, and drugs.
- **Online Shopping** - This option blocks: ecommerce, shopping, and online auctions.

- **Violence** - This option blocks: aggressive content, guns, violence, and weapons.
- **Gambling** - This option blocks: gambling.
- **Identity Protection** - This option blocks: sites that may attempt to gather your personal information or show unwanted pop-ups.

After choosing one or more of these options, you can click the Save button to save and activate the filter; however if you change your mind and do not want to save the changes to the filter, simply click Cancel.

Primary User Options

If you are the **primary user**, you have extra options that allow you to set the filter for other users.

Select User

If there is more than one user on your device, this drop down menu will appear. Using this drop down menu, you can choose between users in order to set the filter for them. Additionally, you can use the Lock Settings: check box to prevent them from removing these settings.

Set As Default

Located to the left of the Save button is the Set As Default button. This button uses the currently selected filter options & activates them in **Guest Mode** and for newly created users.

Importing Favorites

If you have favorites saved on your old PC or Mac computer, you can **export** and **transfer** them to your new computer then use the *Import Favorites* button to add them to your **Favorites**. Instructions on how to export and transfer from your old computer are listed below. The following instructions are for the most recent version of the following web browsers: Internet Explorer, Mozilla Firefox, Google Chrome, and Safari.

Exporting for PC

Listed below are the instructions for exporting Favorites from the following web browsers on a PC. If you have a Mac computer, skip to the section labeled **Exporting for Mac**. When you have finished exporting your Favorites, go to the section labeled **Transferring for PC**.

Exporting from Internet Explorer

1. If you used Internet Explorer, follow these instructions:
2. Open *Internet Explorer* on your old PC.
3. Click the **Favorites** button.
4. Click the down arrow to the right of the **Add to Favorite** button.
5. Click on **Import and Export**.
6. Click **Export to a File**.
7. Click the check box to the word **Favorites**, and then click **Next**.

8. Select the Favorites folder that you want to export. If you want to export all Favorites, select the top level Favorites folder. Otherwise, select the individual folder that you want to export.
9. Click **Next.**
10. By default, Internet Explorer will save the file as **bookmark.htm** in your Documents folder. If you want to use a name other than bookmark.htm, or if you want to store the exported Favorites in a folder other than the Documents folder, go to step 10. If not, skip to step 12.
11. Click **Browse**. Then choose a new file name and/or storage location.
12. When you have chosen a new file name and/or storage location, click **Save**.
13. Click Export.
14. Click Finish.

Exporting from Mozilla Firefox

1. If you used Mozilla Firefox, follow these instructions:
2. Open ***Mozilla Firefox*** on your old PC.
3. Click the **Bookmarks** button on the right side of the navigation toolbar.
4. Click **Show All Bookmarks**.
5. When the popup loads, click the **Import and Backup** button.
6. From the drop-down menu, click **Export Bookmarks to HTML....**
7. By default, Mozilla Firefox will save the file as **bookmarks.html** in your Downloads folder. If you want to use a name other than bookmarks.html, or if you want to store the exported Favorites in a folder other than the Downloads folder, type a different name and/or change the storage location. If not, skip this step.
8. Regardless of whether you decided to change the file name and/or location, click **Save**.

Exporting from Google Chrome

If you used Google Chrome, follow these instructions:

1. Open ***Google Chrome*** on your old PC.
2. Click the Wrench icon on the right side of the browser toolbar.
3. In the drop-down menu, place you cursor on top of the word **Bookmarks**. This will open a second menu to the left of the first.
4. From the second menu, click **Bookmark Manager**. Alternatively, pressing **ctrl**, **Shift**, and **O** simultaneously on your keyboard will also open the **Bookmark Manager**.
5. Once the Bookmark Manager loads, click **Organize**.
6. In the drop-down menu, click **Export bookmarks to HTML file....**
7. By default, Google Chrome will save the file as **bookmarks_A_BB_CC.html** (A represents the month, BB represents the day, and CC represents the last two digits of the year) in your Documents folder. If you want to use a name other than

bookmarks_A_BB_CC.html, or if you want to store the exported Favorites in a folder other than the Documents folder, type a different name and/or change the storage location. If not, skip this step.
8. Regardless of whether you decided to change the file name and/or location, click **Save**.

Exporting from Safari
If you used Safari, follow these instructions:
1. Open **Safari** on your old PC.
2. Click the **File** button, located in the top left corner. If the **File** button is not visible, use the following instructions before moving on to step 3:
   a) Click the Gear icon on the right side of the browser toolbar.
   b) In the drop-down menu, click **Show Menu Bar**.
3. In the drop-down menu, click **Export Bookmarks…**.
4. By default, Safari will save the file as **Safari Bookmarks.html** in your Documents folder. If you want to use a name other than Safari bookmarks.html, or if you want to store the exported Favorites in a folder other than the Documents folder, type a different name and/or change the storage location. If not, skip this step.
5. Regardless of whether you decided to change the file name and/or location, click **Save**.

Exporting for Mac
Listed below are the instructions for exporting Favorites from the following web browsers on a Mac. If you have a PC, scroll up to the section labeled **Exporting for PC**. When you have finished exporting your Favorites, go to the section labeled **Transferring for Mac**.

Transferring from PC
Now that you have your Favorites saved as a file, you can transfer them to your new computer by one of two ways, **Email** or **USB**. The instructions for each method are listed below. When you have finished transferring your Favorites file, go to the section labeled **Using the Import Favorites Button**.

Transferring via Email
1. On your PC, open your web browser.
2. Go to the website of your email provider. For example, if your email address is xxxxxxxx@gmail.com, you would go to www.gmail.com.
3. Open a new email, and put your email address in the **To:** field.
4. Attach your Favorites file to the email.
5. Send the email.
6. On your new computer, go to the *Email* application.
7. Open the email you just sent to yourself. If the email is not present in your Inbox, click the **Refresh Mail** button.

8. Once you have opened the email, click the **View Attachments** button.
9. When the attachment viewer loads, click the **Save** button.
10. When the Save File popup loads, click the **Save** button.

Now that you have your Favorites saved as a file, you can transfer them to your new computer by one of two ways, **Email** or **USB**. The instructions for each method are listed below. When you have finished transferring your Favorites file, go to the section labeled **Using the Import Favorites Button**.

Transferring via Email

1. On your Mac, open your web browser.
2. Go to the website of your email provider. For example, if your email address is xxxxxxxx@gmail.com, you would go to www.gmail.com.
3. Open a new email, and put your email address in the **To:** field.
4. Attach your Favorites file to the email.
5. Send the email.
6. On your new computer, go to the *Email* application.
7. Open the email you just sent to yourself. If the email is not present in your Inbox, click the **Refresh Mail** button.
8. Once you have opened the email, click the **View Attachments** button.
9. When the attachment viewer loads, click the **Save** button.
10. When the Save File popup loads, click the **Save** button.

Transferring via USB

Using the Import Favorites Button

Now that you have your Favorites file saved on your computer, follow these instructions to import them to the Web application's Favorites page:

1. Click the **Web** button on the left side of the screen.
2. Click the **Settings** button, located in the upper right-hand corner of the screen.
3. Click the **Import Favorites** button, located in the upper right-hand corner of the page.
4. A dialog box will appear on the screen telling you that you must have the bookmarks file saved on your computer and asking you if you wish to proceed. Click **Yes**.
5. Click the **Documents** folder.
6. Find the Favorites file and click on it.
7. After selecting the favorites file, click the **Open** button.
8. A dialog box will appear informing you that you favorites have been successfully imported.

After you Favorites have been successfully imported, you can access them via the Favorites button in the Web application.

Wiping the Browser Cache and Cookies

As you navigate to different websites, these websites may store pieces of information on your computer, called cookies, so that they can do things like load faster or remember that you were logged in.

Wipe Cache

Sometimes if you have problems with a website, it may ask you to clear the cache or cookies. To do this, simply press the **Wipe Cache** button. This will delete all cached information and "cookies" from your web browser. Any websites that you were logged into will now "forget" that you were logged in and you will have to login again the next time you visit the website.

Telikin Standard Product Warranty

General Terms and Conditions -Venture 3 Systems LLC., hereunder "V3", offers a Twelve (12) months limited warranty on Telikin Touch 18,5" and Telikin Elite 20", All-in-one PCs, hereunder "Product" from the original date of purchase. The limited warranty is under no circumstances transferable to any other party that is not the original buyer of the Product. This limited warranty only covers the Product that is purchased in the United States and Canada.

Venture 3 Systems LLC (V3) will repair or by any other efforts restore the defective Product to its working condition as originally configured by V3. V3 is not responsible for any subsequent installation by any third party or by the owner. V3 may provide refurbished equipment to restore product to original working condition.

Limited Warranty - Within the valid limited warranty period applied to the Product, Customer may contact V3 for warranty service only when the Product purchased becomes defective under proper usage, the limited warranty is under no circumstances transferable to any other party that is not the original buyer of the Product. The limited warranty DOES NOT cover Cosmetic damages, damage or loss to, data, or removable storage media, or damage due to the following;

1. Acts of God, accident, misuse, abuse, negligence, commercial use or modifications of the Product;
2. Improper operation or maintenance of the Product;
3. Connection to improper voltage supply;
4. Attempted or unauthorized repair by any party other than V3.
5. The warranty seals have been broken or altered.

The limited warranty DOES NOT apply when the malfunction results from the use of the Product in conjunction with accessories, products or ancillary or peripheral equipment, or where it is determined by V3 that there is no fault with the Product itself.

V3 is ONLY responsible for the Telikin branded product purchased in the United States and Canada. The limited warranty service is not, in any way, applicable for any OS or software configured in the Product. Customer's dated sales receipt, showing the original date of purchase of the product is customer's proof of purchase. Customer may be requested by V3 to provide the proof of purchase of the Product when attempting to make use of the limited warranty service.

The following items (inclusive but not limited to) are covered under this warranty.

CPU, HDD, MEMORY, MOTHERBOARD, TOUCH SCREEN, SPEAKERS, DVD/CD, LCD PANEL, WIRELESS MODULE, MICROPHONE, WEBCAM, POWER ADAPTER.

Accessories (inclusive but not limited to), such as keyboard and mouse, are not covered by warranty, except DOA (Dead on arrival). Claims for DOA keyboards, or mice must be submitted within 1 month of purchase date.

LCD (Liquid Crystal Display) Screen Bad Pixel Policy: -All of all-in-one PC displays use TFT* technology, manufactured according to high industry standards, to guarantee trouble-free personal computing. Nevertheless, your display may have a cosmetic imperfection that appears as small bright or dark spots. This is common to all LCD displays and cannot be avoided by any of our models. These imperfections are caused by one or more defective pixels. V3 warrants a defective LCD display as having 7 or more "Dead" pixels, where a dead pixel is a black dot. "Stuck" pixels are Red, Green or Blue dots that often correct themselves with time. Customers should contact the original retail store where the Telikin was purchased or V3 within 30 days from the invoice date for a replacement.

Labor - Within the limited warranty period applied to the Product, V3 will repair defects in the Product at no charge. After the limited warranty period applied to the Product, Customer can choose to have the Product repaired on a fee basis. The Customer may also choose to purchase an extended warranty. See Extended warranty terms.

Parts - Within the limited warranty period applied to the Product, V3 will repair or replace the defective parts of the Product. After the limited warranty period applied to the Product, Customer can choose to have the parts of the Product to be repaired or replaced on a fee basis. The Customer may also choose to purchase an extended warranty. See Extended warranty terms.

Protection / Back-Up of Stored Data - Unless the Customer has purchased the VIP Support program, which includes automatic network backup, it is Customer's responsibility to back up the contents of your hard drive, including any data you have stored on the hard drive. The VIP Support program can be purchased directly from your Telikin computer by going to "MORE", "BACKUP/RESTORE", and pressing the "Sign Up Now" button, or by calling 1-800-730-6893.

IF DURING THE REPAIR OF THE PRODUCT THE CONTENTS OF THE HARD DRIVE ARE ALTERED, DELETED, OR IN ANYWAY MODIFIED, V3 IS NOT RESPONSIBLE WHATSOEVER. CUSTOMER'S PRODUCT WILL BE RETUNRED AS ORIGINALLY CONFIGURED WHEN MANUFACT URED/PURCHASED.

Telikin Extended Warranty - 2 additional Years coverage to the 1 year Standard Warranty

  $99.00 – 18.5" Telikin Touch $129.00 – 20" Telikin Elite

How to Purchase Extended Warranty - All end users who purchase Telikin Branded (e.g. Telikin Touch 18.5", or Telikin Elite 20") must register products prior to purchasing the extended warranty. You can register your product from the "Please register your Product" notice in the 'Notices' panel on the "HOME" page. Once valid serial numbers are entered during product registration, end users will be eligible to purchase the extended warranty. This warranty policy DOES NOT apply to accessories such as Keyboard, mice, external speakers, headphones, and printers.

The Following items (inclusive but not limited to) are covered under this warranty.

CPU, HDD, MEMORY, MOTHERBOARD, TOUCH SCREEN, SPEAKERS, DVD/CD, LCD PANEL, WIRELESS MODULE, MICROPHONE, WEBCAM and POWER ADAPTER

Terms and Conditions:

The Warranty Extension Service must be purchased within the 90 days of the original purchase date. (The purchase invoice or other proof of purchase is required.) The Warranty Extension Service DOES NOT cover Cosmetic damages (scratches, dents…etc.), lost, stolen, incorrect or inadequate custom installation, intentional damage, recovery or transfer data, act of God or nature.

The Warranty Extension Service only covers failures or malfunctions that occur during the warranty period and under normal use conditions, as well as any material or workmanship defects. The warranty will not apply if:

The user is unable to provide proof of warranty and/or proof of purchase

The warranty seals have been broken or altered

The product has been tampered, repaired and/or modified by non-Venture 3 Systems (V3) Service Technician.

Damages due to use outside of the operation or storage parameters or environment detailed in the Quick Start Guide, or built-in HELP files or Videos.

The serial number on the Telikin has been altered, cancelled or removed

Damage caused by improper installation or improper connection to a peripheral device

Damage caused by accident, natural disaster, intentional or accidental misuse, abuse, neglect or improper maintenance, or use under abnormal conditions

Damages resulting from a malicious network attack or Virus.

The Warranty Extension Service can only be purchased and applies to products purchased in the United States and Canada.

V3 will only cover the one-way ground shipping from the point of service back to the user's location.

Extended Warranty is non-transferable to any other party that is not the original buyer of the Product.

Extended Warranty purchase is NOT refundable.

Customer must contact V3 technical support and obtain a RA number from V3 prior to returning the defective Product. Customer needs to return the defect Product to V3 within 15 days from the RA issuance date. Failing to do so may prevent customer from being eligible for the issued RA number and thus Customer may need to request another RA number.

In the case of specific part which is no longer manufactured, the then current closest functionally equivalent Replacement Equipment will be used as determined by the V3 technician.

End User License Agreement (EULA)

IMPORTANT: PLEASE READ THE TERMS AND CONDITIONS OF THIS LICENSE AGREEMENT CAREFULLY BEFORE USING THIS PRODUCT. Venture 3 Systems LLC ("Company") End-User License Agreement ("EULA") is a legal agreement between you (either an individual or a single entity) and Company for SOFTWARE identified above which may include associated software components, media, videos, printed materials, and "online" or electronic documentation ("SOFTWARE"). By installing, copying, or otherwise using the SOFTWARE, you agree to be bound by the terms of this EULA. This license agreement represents the entire agreement concerning the program between you and Company, (referred to as "licenser"), and it supersedes any prior proposal, representation, or understanding between the parties. If you do not agree to the terms of this EULA, do not install or use the SOFTWARE. The SOFTWARE is protected by copyright laws and international copyright treaties, as well as other intellectual property laws and treaties. The SOFTWARE is licensed, not sold.

1. GRANT OF LICENSE.
The SOFTWARE is licensed for use on one computer.

2. DESCRIPTION OF OTHER RIGHTS AND LIMITATIONS.

   a. You must not remove or alter any copyright notices on any and all copies of the SOFTWARE.
   b. You may not distribute registered copies of the SOFTWARE to third parties.
   c. You may not reverse engineer, decompile, or disassemble the SOFTWARE.
   d. You may not rent, lease, or lend the SOFTWARE.
   e. You must comply with all applicable laws regarding use of the SOFTWARE.

3. TERMINATION
Without prejudice to any other rights, Company may terminate this EULA if you fail to comply with the terms and conditions of this EULA. In such event, you must return or destroy all copies of the SOFTWARE in your possession.

4. COPYRIGHT
All title, including but not limited to copyrights, in and to the SOFTWARE and any copies thereof are owned by Company. All title and intellectual property rights in and to the content which may be accessed through use of the SOFTWARE is the property of the respective content owner and may be protected by applicable copyright or other intellectual property laws and treaties. This EULA grants you no rights to use such content. All rights not expressly granted are reserved by Company.

5. NO WARRANTIES
The SOFTWARE is provided "As Is" without any express or implied warranty of any kind, including but not limited to any warranties of merchantability, no infringement, or fitness of a particular purpose. Company does not warrant or assume responsibility for the accuracy or completeness of any information, text, graphics, links or other items contained within the SOFTWARE. Company makes no warranties respecting any harm that may be caused by the transmission of a computer virus, worm, time bomb, logic bomb, or other such computer program.

6. LIMITATION OF LIABILITY
In no event shall Company be liable for any damages (including, without limitation, lost profits, business interruption, or lost information) rising out of "Authorized Users" use of or inability to use the SOFTWARE, even if Company has been advised of the possibility of such damages. In no event will Company be liable for loss of data or for indirect, special,

incidental, consequential (including lost profit), or other damages based in contract, tort or otherwise. Company shall have no liability with respect to the content of the SOFTWARE or any part thereof, including but not limited to errors or omissions contained therein, libel, infringements of rights of publicity, privacy, trademark rights, business interruption, personal injury, loss of privacy, moral rights or the disclosure of confidential information.

7. OPEN SOURCE LICENSE NOTICES
The following are notices compliant with software libraries included in this product.

Log4j, Google Data Java Client, Google Guava Library, Android V-Card, Soap, XMLBeans, OpenCSV, HTTPComponents, HttpClient are licensed under the Apache Software License, Version 2.0 www.apache.org/licenses/LICENSE-2.0

Mozilla Libraries, Saxon, and IcePDF are licensed under the Mozilla Public License MPL v1.1 www.mozilla.org/MPL/MPL-1.1.html

JavaMail: is licensed from Oracle JavaMail(TM) API 1.4.3 www.java.com/en/download/license.jsp

Appframework, DJNativeSwing, JNA and Beansbinding are licensed under the GNU Lesser General Public License 2.1 LGPL-2.1 www.opensource.org/licenses/lgpl-2.1.php, Source code available at www.telikin.com/open_source.php

TinyCore Linux, the Linux kernel, and various other binaries distributed on this product are licensed under the GNU General Public License Version 2 GPL v2 www.gnu.org/licenses/gpl-2.0.html, Source code available at www.telikin.com/open_source.php

LibreOffice Libraries are licensed under the GNU Lesser General Public Library LGPL v3 www.opensource.org/licenses/lgpl-3.0, Source code available at www.telikin.com/open_source.php

JXLayer, TimingFramework, and AnimatedTransitions are licensed under the BSD License. www.freebsd.org/copyright/license.html

XStream: BSD License Copyright (c) 2003-2006, Joe Walnes, Copyright (c) 2006-2007, XStream Committers All rights reserved.

- Redistribution and use in source and binary forms, with or without modification, are permitted provided that the following conditions are met:
- Redistributions of source code must retain the above copyright notice, this list of conditions and the following disclaimer. Redistributions in binary form must reproduce the above copyright notice, this list of conditions and the following disclaimer in the documentation and/or other materials provided with the distribution.
- Neither the name of XStream nor the names of its contributors may be used to endorse or promote products derived from this software without specific prior written permission.

THIS SOFTWARE IS PROVIDED BY THE COPYRIGHT HOLDERS AND CONTRIBUTORS "AS IS" AND ANY EXPRESS OR IMPLIED WARRANTIES, INCLUDING, BUT NOT LIMITED TO, THE IMPLIED WARRANTIES OF MERCHANTABILITY AND FITNESS FOR A PARTICULAR PURPOSE ARE DISCLAIMED. IN NO EVENT SHALL THE COPYRIGHT OWNER OR CONTRIBUTORS BE LIABLE FOR ANY DIRECT, INDIRECT, INCIDENTAL, SPECIAL, EXEMPLARY, OR CONSEQUENTIAL DAMAGES (INCLUDING, BUT NOT LIMITED TO, PROCUREMENT OF SUBSTITUTE GOODS OR SERVICES; LOSS OF USE, DATA, OR PROFITS; OR BUSINESS INTERRUPTION) HOWEVER CAUSED AND ON ANY THEORY OF LIABILITY, WHETHER IN CONTRACT, STRICT LIABILITY, OR TORT (INCLUDING NEGLIGENCE OR OTHERWISE) ARISING IN ANY WAY OUT OF THE USE OF THIS SOFTWARE, EVEN IF ADVISED OF THE POSSIBILITY OF SUCH DAMAGE.

Xpp3: Version 1.1.1 www.extreme.indiana.edu/xgws/xsoap/xpp/ Copyright (c) 2002 Extreme! Lab, Indiana University. All rights reserved. "This product includes software developed by the Indiana University Extreme! Lab www.extreme.indiana.edu" THIS SOFTWARE IS PROVIDED "AS IS" AND ANY EXPRESSED OR IMPLIED WARRANTIES, INCLUDING, BUT NOT LIMITED TO, THE IMPLIED WARRANTIES OF MERCHANTABILITY AND FITNESS FOR A PARTICULAR PURPOSE ARE DISCLAIMED. IN NO EVENT SHALL THE AUTHORS,

COPYRIGHT HOLDERS OR ITS CONTRIBUTORS BE LIABLE FOR ANY DIRECT, INDIRECT, INCIDENTAL, SPECIAL, EXEMPLARY, OR CONSEQUENTIAL DAMAGES (INCLUDING, BUT NOT LIMITED TO, PROCUREMENT OF SUBSTITUTE GOODS OR SERVICES; LOSS OF USE, DATA, OR PROFITS; OR BUSINESS INTERRUPTION) HOWEVER CAUSED AND ON ANY THEORY OF LIABILITY, WHETHER IN CONTRACT, STRICT LIABILITY, OR TORT (INCLUDING NEGLIGENCE OR OTHERWISE) ARISING IN ANY WAY OUT OF THE USE OF THIS SOFTWARE, EVEN IF ADVISED OF THE POSSIBILITY OF SUCH DAMAGE.

ICal4J: Copyright (c) 2011, Ben Fortuna All rights reserved. Redistribution and use in source and binary forms, with or without modification, are permitted provided that the following conditions are met:

- Redistributions of source code must retain the above copyright notice, this list of conditions and the following disclaimer.
- Redistributions in binary form must reproduce the above copyright notice, this list of conditions and the following disclaimer in the documentation and/or other materials provided with the distribution.
- Neither the name of Ben Fortuna nor the names of any other contributors may be used to endorse or promote products derived from this software without specific prior written permission.

THIS SOFTWARE IS PROVIDED BY THE COPYRIGHT HOLDERS AND CONTRIBUTORS "AS IS" AND ANY EXPRESS OR IMPLIED WARRANTIES, INCLUDING, BUT NOT LIMITED TO, THE IMPLIED WARRANTIES OF MERCHANTABILITY AND FITNESS FOR A PARTICULAR PURPOSE ARE DISCLAIMED. IN NO EVENT SHALL THE COPYRIGHT OWNER OR CONTRIBUTORS BE LIABLE FOR ANY DIRECT, INDIRECT, INCIDENTAL, SPECIAL, EXEMPLARY, OR CONSEQUENTIAL DAMAGES (INCLUDING, BUT NOT LIMITED TO, PROCUREMENT OF SUBSTITUTE GOODS OR SERVICES; LOSS OF USE, DATA, OR PROFITS; OR BUSINESS INTERRUPTION) HOWEVER CAUSED AND ON ANY THEORY OF LIABILITY, WHETHER IN CONTRACT, STRICT LIABILITY, OR TORT (INCLUDING NEGLIGENCE OR OTHERWISE) ARISING IN ANY WAY OUT OF THE USE OF THIS SOFTWARE, EVEN IF ADVISED OF THE POSSIBILITY OF SUCH DAMAGE.

Java Pdf Extraction Decoding Access Library:

Project Info: http://www.jpedal.org (C) Copyright 1997-2008, IDRsolutions and Contributors. Main Developer: Simon Barnett

Copyright (c) 2008, IDRsolutions All rights reserved.

Redistribution and use in source and binary forms, with or without modification, are permitted provided that the following conditions are met:

- Redistributions of source code must retain the above copyright notice, this list of conditions and the following disclaimer.
- Redistributions in binary form must reproduce the above copyright notice, this list of conditions and the following disclaimer in the documentation and/or other materials provided with the distribution.
- Neither the name of the IDRsolutions nor the names of its contributors may be used to endorse or promote products derived from this software without specific prior written permission.

THIS SOFTWARE IS PROVIDED BY THE COPYRIGHT HOLDERS AND CONTRIBUTORS "AS IS" AND ANY EXPRESS OR IMPLIED WARRANTIES, INCLUDING, BUT NOT LIMITED TO, THE IMPLIED WARRANTIES OF MERCHANTABILITY AND FITNESS FOR A PARTICULAR PURPOSE ARE DISCLAIMED. IN NO EVENT SHALL THE COPYRIGHT OWNER OR CONTRIBUTORS BE LIABLE FOR ANY DIRECT, INDIRECT, INCIDENTAL, SPECIAL, EXEMPLARY, OR CONSEQUENTIAL DAMAGES (INCLUDING, BUT NOT LIMITED TO, PROCUREMENT OF SUBSTITUTE GOODS OR SERVICES; LOSS OF USE, DATA, OR PROFITS; OR BUSINESS INTERRUPTION) HOWEVER CAUSED AND ON ANY THEORY OF LIABILITY, WHETHER IN CONTRACT, STRICT LIABILITY, OR TORT (INCLUDING NEGLIGENCE OR OTHERWISE) ARISING IN ANY WAY OUT OF THE USE OF THIS SOFTWARE, EVEN IF ADVISED OF THE POSSIBILITY OF SUCH DAMAGE.

Other JBIG2 image decoding implementations include jbig2dec (http://jbig2dec.sourceforge.net/) xpdf (http://www.foolabs.com/xpdf/)

The final draft JBIG2 specification can be found at http://www.jpeg.org/public/fcd14492.pdf

All three of the above resources were used in the writing of this software, with methodologies, processes and inspiration taken from all three.

Java Pdf CCITTFax Decoding Library:

Based on the SUN code (see license beyond) changes are made to handle CCITTFax encoded data in a PDF image. This may or may not apply to real world CCITT documents.

Copyright (c) 2007, intarsys consulting GmbH

Redistribution and use in source and binary forms, with or without modification, are permitted provided that the following conditions are met:

- Redistributions of source code must retain the above copyright notice, this list of conditions and the following disclaimer.
- Redistributions in binary form must reproduce the above copyright notice, this list of conditions and the following disclaimer in the documentation and/or other materials provided with the distribution.
- Neither the name of intarsys nor the names of its contributors may be used to endorse or promote products derived from this software without specific prior written permission.

THIS SOFTWARE IS PROVIDED BY THE COPYRIGHT HOLDERS AND CONTRIBUTORS "AS IS" AND ANY EXPRESS OR IMPLIED WARRANTIES, INCLUDING, BUT NOT LIMITED TO, THE IMPLIED WARRANTIES OF MERCHANTABILITY AND FITNESS FOR A PARTICULAR PURPOSE ARE DISCLAIMED. IN NO EVENT SHALL THE COPYRIGHT OWNER OR CONTRIBUTORS BE LIABLE FOR ANY DIRECT, INDIRECT, INCIDENTAL, SPECIAL, EXEMPLARY, OR CONSEQUENTIAL DAMAGES (INCLUDING, BUT NOT LIMITED TO, PROCUREMENT OF SUBSTITUTE GOODS OR SERVICES; LOSS OF USE, DATA, OR PROFITS; OR BUSINESS INTERRUPTION) HOWEVER CAUSED AND ON ANY THEORY OF LIABILITY, WHETHER IN CONTRACT, STRICT LIABILITY, OR TORT (INCLUDING NEGLIGENCE OR OTHERWISE) ARISING IN ANY WAY OUT OF THE USE OF THIS SOFTWARE, EVEN IF ADVISED OF THE POSSIBILITY OF SUCH DAMAGE.

Copyright (c) 2001 Sun Microsystems, Inc. All Rights Reserved.

Redistribution and use in source and binary forms, with or without modification, are permitted provided that the following conditions are met:

- Redistributions of source code must retain the above copyright notice, this list of conditions and the following disclaimer.
- Redistributions in binary form must reproduce the above copyright notice, this list of conditions and the following disclaimer in the documentation and/or other materials provided with the distribution.
- either the name of Sun Microsystems, Inc. or the names of contributors may be used to endorse or promote products derived from this software without specific prior written permission.

This software is provided "AS IS," without a warranty of any kind. ALL EXPRESS OR IMPLIED CONDITIONS, REPRESENTATIONS AND WARRANTIES, INCLUDING ANY IMPLIED WARRANTY OF MERCHANTABILITY, FITNESS FOR A PARTICULAR PURPOSE OR NON-INFRINGEMENT, ARE HEREBY EXCLUDED. SUN AND ITS LICENSORS SHALL NOT BE LIABLE FOR ANY DAMAGES SUFFERED BY LICENSEE AS A RESULT OF USING, MODIFYING OR DISTRIBUTING THE SOFTWARE OR ITS DERIVATIVES. IN NO EVENT WILL SUN OR ITS LICENSORS BE LIABLE FOR ANY LOST REVENUE, PROFIT OR DATA, OR FOR DIRECT, INDIRECT, SPECIAL, CONSEQUENTIAL, INCIDENTAL OR PUNITIVE DAMAGES, HOWEVER CAUSED AND REGARDLESS OF THE THEORY OF LIABILITY, ARISING OUT OF THE USE OF OR INABILITY TO USE SOFTWARE, EVEN IF SUN HAS BEEN ADVISED OF THE POSSIBILITY OF SUCH DAMAGES.

You acknowledge that Software is not designed, licensed or intended for use in the design, construction, operation or maintenance of any nuclear facility.

Save Your Account Information

Network
  Wireless Network Name (SSID): _____
  Wireless Network Password: _____

Email
  Email Address: _____
  Email Password: _____

Video Chat (Skype)
  Account Username: _____
  Skype Password: _____

Photos (Facebook)
  Facebook Email Address: _____
  Facebook Password: _____

Tech Buddy
Chris Cabot Cummins
cummins.tl@gmail.com

VIP Support 800-730-6893
New Customers 800-730-6893
Standard Support 267-954-0110

Rev #2.8.3